*Child Psychopathology
and the Quest
for Control*

DEVELOPMENTAL CLINICAL PSYCHOLOGY AND PSYCHIATRY SERIES

Series Editor: **Alan E. Kazdin,** *Western Psychiatric Institute*

In the Series:

Child Psychopathology
and the Quest
for Control

FRED ROTHBAUM

JOHN R. WEISZ

Volume 17
Developmental Clinical Psychology and Psychiatry

SAGE PUBLICATIONS
The Publishers of Professional Social Science
Newbury Park   London   New Delhi

For information address:

SAGE Publications, Inc.
2111 West Hillcrest Drive
Newbury Park, California 91320

SAGE Publications Ltd.
28 Banner Street
London EC1Y 8QE
England

SAGE Publications India Pvt. Ltd.
M-32 Market
Greater Kailash I
New Delhi 110 048 India

Printed in the United States of America

Library of Congress Cataloging-in Publication Data

Rothbaum, Fred.
     Child psychopathology and the quest for control.
     (Developmental clinical psychology and psychiatry
series ; v. 17)
     Bibliography: p.
     1. Child psychopathology. I. Weisz, John R.
II. Title.   III. Series: Developmental clinical
psychology and psychiatry ; v. 17. [DNLM: 1. Child
Development. 2. Psychopathology—in infancy & childhood.
W1 DE997NC v. 17 / WS 350 R845c]
RJ499.R665   1988   618.92'89   88-33626
ISBN 0-8039-3147-6
ISBN 0-8039-3148-4 (pbk.)

FIRST PRINTING 1989

CONTENTS

INTRODUCTION TO THE SERIES

Interest in child development and adjustment is by no means new. Yet only recently has the study of children benefitted from advances in both clinical and scientific research. Advances in the social and biological sciences, and the emergence of disciplines and subdisciplines that focus exclusively on childhood and adolescence, and greater appreciation of the impact of such influences as the family, peers, and school have helped accelerate research on developmental psychopathology. Apart from interest in the study of child development and adjustment for its own sake, the need to address clinical problems of adulthood naturally draws one to investigate precursors in childhood and adolescence.

Within a relatively brief period, the study of psychopathology among children and adolescents has proliferated considerably. Several different professional journals, annual book series, and handbooks devoted entirely to the study of children and adolescents and their adjustment document the proliferation of work in the field. Nevertheless, there is a paucity of resource material that presents information in an authoritative, systematic, and disseminable fashion. There is a need within the field to convey the latest developments and to represent different disciplines, approaches and conceptual views to the topics of childhood and adolescent adjustment and maladjustment.

The Sage Series on Developmental Clinical Psychology and Psychiatry is designed to serve uniquely several needs of the field. The series encompasses individual monographs prepared by experts in the fields of clinical child psychology, child psychiatry, child development and related disciplines. The primary focus is on developmental psychopathology, which refers broadly here to the diagnosis, assessment, treatment, and prevention of problems that arise in the period from infancy through adolescence. A working assumption of the series is that understanding, identifying, and treating problems of youth must draw on multiple disciplines and diverse views within a given discipline.

The task for individual contributors is to present the latest theory and research on various topics including specific types of dysfunction, diagnostic and treatment approaches, and special problem areas that affect adjustment. Core topics within clinical work are addressed by the series. Authors are asked to bridge potential theory, research and clinical practice, and to outline the current status and future directions. The goals of the series and the tasks presented to individual contributors are demanding. We have been extremely fortunate in recruiting leaders in the fields who have been able to translate their recognized scholarship and expertise into highly readable works on contemporary topics.

The present book, completed by Drs. Fred Rothbaum and John Weisz, focuses on child psychopathology and the quest for control. The authors examine theory and research on the emergence and development of beliefs among children and adolescents and the expression of these in relation to dysfunction at different ages. The central thesis is that changing views of the child over the course of development lead to significant changes in functional and maladaptive affect and behavior. The notion of control is viewed as an organizing theme upon which both theory and research can be integrated about cognitive processes, motivation, and childhood dysfunction. The book is remarkably broad in its scope by at once drawing upon diverse areas of social, developmental, and clinical psychology, and integrating both theory and research. The excellent interplay of conceptual views and evidence, as well as experimentation, case studies, and everyday experience help convey the emergence of psychopathology from a developmental perspective.

PREFACE

This book examines the influence of cognitive development on child psychopathology. With the recent expansion of research and theory at the interface of these fields, the time seems right to begin preliminary synthesis and to take first steps toward theory construction. Although many of our ideas are speculative, they are grounded in empirical research reviewed herein. We also rely on previous theoretical efforts to synthesize the relevant empirical evidence (e.g., Cowan, 1978; Elkind, 1979; Kegan, 1982; Rosen, 1985; Selman, 1980). Filling in gaps of our model will require substantial new research and further integrative efforts.

Our main goal is to highlight points of convergence in the literature on: (a) developments in children's understanding of control, (b) relations between control beliefs and psychopathology, and (c) the age-related character of many forms of psychopathology. We illustrate the convergence by focusing on problems that peak in incidence at particular age periods. These include negativism and phobias in early childhood, hostile aggression and inferiority in middle childhood, and rebellion and depression in adolescence. In tracing connections between the development of these problems and children's control beliefs, we borrow from other control-based theories.

In early childhood, conceptions of control are magical in several ways. Preschool children attribute causal influence to their own wishes, to arbitrary rituals, and to unseen imaginary forces. Negativism can be sparked when the young child's efforts to achieve magical control are thwarted. Phobias can develop when aversive outcomes are ascribed to malevolent imaginary agents.

In middle childhood, control concepts focus on one's potential and power relative to others'. When others threaten to manifest superior potential or more potent power, the child may take preventative action, in the form of hostile aggression. By contrast, impressions that others have overwhelming superiority in potential or power can coalesce into persistent feelings of inferiority.

In adolescence control concepts are intertwined with the concept of freedom—the ability to take action and make decisions that are not bound by arbitrary systems. Rebellion is often fueled by the belief that freedom requires defying the constraints of the existing system. Depression can be fueled by the belief that freedom and desirable outcomes are unobtainable, and that this will be true in the future.

At each stage of childhood we describe psychological problems and we seek to explain the development of these problems in terms of evolving cognitive processes—specifically, evolving beliefs about control. Finally, we consider two related issues: (a) relations between control beliefs and hormonal, environmental and other cognitive developmental determinants of children's psychological problems, and (b) methods of testing our model and its hypotheses.

We wish to thank the following individuals for their helpful comments regarding earlier drafts of this manuscript: Tom Achenbach, Gus Blasi, Charles Carver, Mark Dix, David Elkind, Marilou Hyson, Rachael Karniol, John Nicholls, Gil Noam, Evelyn Pitcher, Diane Ruble, Carolyn Shantz, Charles Wenar and Robert White.

Special thanks are extended to Martha Pott for her excellent thoughtful revisions and to Alan Kazdin for his constructive feedback at all stages of the preparation process. We also thank the children—our own and others'—who have helped us to understand their world.

PART I

INTRODUCTION

1

PSYCHOLOGICAL PROBLEMS[1] AND THE DEVELOPMENT OF CONTROL BELIEFS

PSYCHOLOGICAL PROBLEMS AND COGNITIVE DEVELOPMENT

Some children seem to invite victimization. The pattern is depicted in myriad ways by the fictional character Charlie Brown. In one cartoon, Charlie is the only player on his team to show up for a baseball game during a steady rain. As usual, his teammate Lucy rewards Charlie's loyalty with a hostile aggressive evaluation: "Only a blockhead would be out on a day like this" (Schulz, 1966). In this book, we examine problem behaviors such as Charlie Brown's self-victimization and Lucy's hostile aggression. We focus on other problems too—problems that can also be illustrated by other characters in popular culture. In the movie *Annie Hall,* Woody Allen exemplifies a depressed perspective in such quotes as "Life is divided up into the horrible and the miserable. Those are the two categories. The horrible would be like terminal cases and blind people, cripples. I don't know how they get through life. It's amazing to me. And the miserable is everyone else." Jack Nicholson, another film comedian, displays starkly different psychological problems—most often, outrageous rebellion. In the movie *Five Easy Pieces* he is irritated by a small-minded waitress who refuses to serve him a side order of toast because the menu mentions toast only with sandwiches. In a rising crescendo of rage he instructs her to give him a chicken salad sandwich with "no mayonnaise, no butter, no lettuce . . . now all you have to do is hold the chicken . . . hold it between . . .", and ends his profane outburst by using his arm to clear the table of its contents.

We will focus in this book on problems grouped into two broad categories: internalizing (e.g., passive, withdrawn, fearful) problems and externalizing (e.g., hostile, aggressive, disobedient) problems. This distinction, which emerges from numerous factor analytic studies, roughly corresponds to the distinction between functioning that induces suffering in the self and functioning that induces suffering in others (see Achenbach, 1982; Peterson, 1961). Charlie Brown's repeated attempts to kick a football that Lucy consistently removes just as he kicks, and Woody Allen's obsession with death are examples of internalizing problems. Lucy's manipulative attempts to abuse others at her "Psychiatric Help" stand, and Jack Nicholson's relentless defiance of societal institutions are examples of externalizing problems.

How are we to account for psychological problems? Why do some individuals function in ways that lead to suffering when comparable others in similar circumstances do not? Freud emphasized the role of primary process thought—an irrational, impulse-driven mode of viewing the world—in the development of psychopathology. Movement from primary to secondary process thought—a more logical, objective mode of viewing reality—is accompanied by increased mental health. More recently, analytically oriented authors have linked object constancy and other cognitive-developments derived from Piagetian theory to fundamental aspects of socioemotional development, such as separation/individuation and fantasy-reality differentiation (e.g., Anthony, 1976; Blatt, 1974; Greenspan & Lourie, 1981; Wolff, 1960). Research by neobehaviorists has supported the claim that deficits and delays in cognitive development play a role in the etiology of a variety of psychological problems (Bandura, 1981; Meichenbaum, 1977). Limitations in planfulness, covert rehearsal, attention and memory have all been implicated in problem behavior.

Developmentalists concerned with child clinical problems also emphasize the role of deficits and delays. Werner (1957), for example, posited a close connection between cognitive immaturity and psychopathological functioning. More recently there is empirical evidence of links between clinical problems and (a) immature conceptions of self and others (e.g., Noam, Kohlberg, & Snarey, 1983; Selman, 1980), (b) limited ability to adopt the perspective of others (e.g., Elkind, 1979; Flavell, 1968; Selman, 1980), (c) cognitively immature judgments of morality and justice (see Blasi, 1980, and Damon, 1977, for reviews), and deficits in problem solving skills (e.g., Spivak & Shure, 1982).

Since cognitive development is often an uneven process, the cognitive deficit/delay view can help explain problems in specific domains as well as in general functioning. Unevenness, or "décalage," occurs even in impersonal domains, such as when a child displays different levels of understanding of numbers and metaphors. Décalage may be greatest in affectively laden domains, in which the individual is highly motivated to understand better the problem so as to resolve it or, conversely, to not understand (to deny or distort) the problem.

Despite the strengths of the cognitive deficit/delay position, we have a different emphasis. While we agree that cognitive immaturity plays a significant role in psychological problems, we believe that cognitive functioning plays a larger and more complex role than is depicted in the foregoing theories. We agree with Shantz who described the limitation of the foregoing formulations as follows: "The most frequently investigated position is that advanced social cognitive abilities . . . are positively related to the frequency of prosocial behavior and negatively related to the frequency of antisocial behavior. It is unclear . . . why this position is so widely held because social information and understanding . . . can be used for social good or ill" (Shantz, 1983, p. 526; see also White, 1979). A related point, suggested by a few Piagetian investigators, (e.g., Elkind, 1979), is that young children do not simply have *less* understanding than older children have; rather, they have a *different* understanding. It is possible that these differences in understanding contribute to psychological problems as much as do deficits in understanding. By the same token, older children's and adolescents' understanding of their world predisposes them to psychological problems that are not likely at less mature levels of cognitive functioning.

To illustrate this position, consider the following examples. Preschool children manifest phobias not just because of their very primitive skills in detecting true causal influences, but also because of the causal inferences they are able to draw. Unlike toddlers, they can discern abstract, symbolic similarities between outcomes and suspected agents——for example, that both are "bad"——and on that basis they may erroneously infer causality. Depression may also reflect cognitive maturation: It is generally not until adolescence that children are able to contemplate a distant future and systematically to reject possibilities for constructively shaping that future. Ironically then, psychological problems reflect accomplishments as well as deficits in intellectual functioning.

Note that we depict level of cognitive development as making the child susceptible to certain problems rather than as *causing* those problems. For example, preschoolers are more prone to phobias than are children of other ages, but most preschoolers do not experience phobias in most situations. Moreover, children of other ages experience phobias as well (see Wenar, in press). Cognitive development, then, acts as predisposer: it sets the stage for phobias and other problems, making the problems more or less likely at particular ages, but it alone does not determine whether a problem will arise.

To understand how cognitive functioning may predispose children to develop psychological problems, consider the following example. A youngster known to one of the authors once visited an amusement park containing a House of Horrors, populated by rather realistic-looking ghosts. Although he was frightened, his fear quickly subsided upon leaving the House. That evening, the boy spent the night with his father and stepmother. His mother, with whom he usually stayed, had discouraged the overnight visit, vaguely suggesting to her son that some harm might befall him. At bedtime, when he was tucked in, the light turned off, and the bedroom door closed, the boy grew frightened. He fled the bedroom, terrified of "ghosts," and he remained awake and fearful for much of the night. The boy's fear appeared to originate in the vague concerns his mother had expressed, and the unfamiliar circumstances of his father's darkened guest bedroom. But these causes were less salient in the boy's mind, and less obviously "scary," than were the ghosts seen in the House of Horrors. So the boy identified those ghosts as primary causes of his fear. The salience of the temporal connection between the amusement park visit and the unfamiliar bedroom, and the fact that both were aversive, frightening, and associated with the dark, could constitute "proof" of their causal connectedness in the mind of a young child.

Whether immature thinking leads to illogical conclusions and psychological problems or to accurate conclusions and adaptive functioning depends upon a variety of factors. For example, factors contributing to phobias include (a) highly stressful events that are very difficult to comprehend and that involve salient coincidences with other events (as in the preceding example), (b) the individual's reinforcement history (e.g., if the phobic behavior is rewarded), (c) social expectations emanating from the larger culture (e.g., expectations that girls will express fears), (d) influences from the immediate context (e.g., parental expectations that the environment is dangerous or modeling of fearfulness), and (e) biological/constitutional factors, such as a difficult temperament and gender.[2] It is likely that these factors work in tandem with cognitive functioning.

One of the ways the foregoing factors influence problems is by shaping the specific *content* of children's beliefs. This content, in turn, influences the style (Rothbaum, 1980; Rothbaum et al., 1982; Wortman & Brehm, 1975) and intensity (Wortman & Brehm, 1975) of psychological problems. For example, grade-schoolers who have repeatedly experienced failure are likely to attribute failure in new situations to lack of ability and, as a result, to manifest helplessness (see Dweck & Elliott, 1983, for a review). Grade-schoolers' tendency to make ability attributions reflects their *level* of cognitive functioning (Nicholls, 1978), but the specific content of their ability attributions reflects various factors, including prior failure. The point is that specific problems reflect specific beliefs (e.g., helplessness reflects low ability attributions), and level of cognitive functioning is but one of several factors predisposing specific beliefs.

THE QUEST FOR CONTROL

In explaining the development of children's problems, we highlight the child's quest for control. We define control as causal influence in an intended direction (see Skinner & Chapman, 1983; Weisz, 1986a).[3] Only recently have researchers begun to document the depth and pervasiveness of the desire for control, and the diversity of manifestations of this desire. As noted by Bandura, theory and research on clinical problems have been "mainly concerned with people's hopes for favorable outcomes . . . rather than with their sense of personal mastery" (1977, p. 194). White (1979) attributes this neglect of control (which he refers to alternately as "control" and "competence") to the fact that it is often intermingled with other, more visible, motives.

> Trying to exert influence is . . . mingled with other needs, to be fed, comforted, helped, supported, loved and esteemed. We find it difficult to distinguish the element of competence, of being able to have an influence, from these other needs to which it is instrumental. (White, 1979, p. 10)

Perhaps it is the pervasiveness of control that makes it so difficult to detect. Unlike "drives" that manifest themselves in brief bursts of energy, control motivation is a chronic condition. When not intensely directed toward specific instrumental ends, it is seen in such everyday behaviors as play, exploration and exercise (see White, 1960). It is so much a part of our lives that we have difficulty stepping back and taking stock of it. The aphorism "The fish are the last to discover the ocean" often applies to people's discovery of their desire for control.

While the pervasiveness of control motivation has been increasingly recognized in recent years, its contribution to the development of psychopathology is still not widely appreciated (see Bandura, 1977; Garmezy, Masten, Nordstrom, & Ferrerese, 1979; White, 1979). According to White (1960), models of psychopathology miss "significant problems of growth. In particular, they fail to recognize the development of competence" (p. 99), which is required for the individual's "maintaining itself, growing and flourishing" (p. 100). For example, investigators often neglect the fact that frustration of the desire for control plays a prominent role in many traumatic crises, such as illness and loss of motility due to accidents (i.e., diminished ability to manipulate the physical environment), peer rejection, failure in sports activities, and failure at school (Rothbaum, 1980).

The purpose of this book is to describe and document the contribution of control. Our position is that *at each stage of intellectual development, children are predisposed to certain kinds of problems and protected from others because of their beliefs about, and desire for, control.* Control is adopted as an organizing theme in the present model because it bridges cognitive-developmental and motivational considerations. That is, control refers both to a network of evolving beliefs *and* to a complex motivational system involving such desires as autonomy, industry, mastery, power, and freedom.

We emphasize control even though there are certainly other important motives involved in psychopathology and adaptation. As noted by White (1960, p. 137):

> A person developed wholly along lines of competence, with no dimensions of passion, love or friendliness, would never qualify for maturity. Competence is not intended to describe such experiences as enjoying food, immersing oneself in a sexual relationship, loving children, cherishing friends, being moved by natural beauty or great works of art; nor is it designed to swallow up the problems created by aggression and anxiety.

While control must take its place alongside other motives, we regard the influence of control as one of the most pervasive and least understood of the powerful incentives shaping the child's psychological problems.

FROM MAGIC TO POWER TO FREEDOM

The following overview of control beliefs draws very selectively from empirical literature. Later we provide a fuller review of the relevant evidence on causality and intentionality—two components of control.

Control as magic. "Magical control" refers to young children's (ages 2-6) limited comprehension of processes leading from causes to outcomes.[4] Instead of assuming the existence of mediating events that can be objectively explored, preschoolers often assume that connections between events are immediate and automatic, or they invoke supernatural agents (e.g., Santa Claus, the tooth fairy, monsters) to explain the connections (Piaget, 1930). For example, they assume that punishments automatically follow from wrongdoing rather than searching out natural forces mediating between misdeed and punishment (Piaget, 1948). Preschoolers experience particular difficulty when reasoning about causes that cannot be seen, for example, the unobservable processes operating in magic tricks and in natural phenomena, such as evaporation (Koutsourais, 1984). Moreover, they sometimes assume that the fate of external objects and events is determined by various thoughts (e.g., wishes) and actions (e.g., not stepping on cracks in the sidewalk) that, in reality, have no influence over the outcome.

Young children generally do not fall prey to belief in magical control when the event sequences are relatively simple, repeatedly observed or experienced, and very concrete, and when the children are not required to rely extensively on their memory or verbal skills (see Sedlak & Kurtz, 1981). Belief in magical control, when it does appear, seems often to result from reliance on salient, observable causal explanations rather than logical, unobservable ones. Moreover, young children often assume an automatic connection between intentions and outcomes.

Control as power. The term *power,* as used here, refers to the awareness of the potential to influence outcomes, as opposed to the belief that outcomes occur immediately and automatically. Understanding of power involves recognition of mediating events, of probability, and of abstract causes like individual capability.

Grade school children recognize cases in which one force influences another, which influences another, in an ongoing progression. For example, social status is not necessarily desired for immediate or specific outcomes but for the potential control it implies. These outcomes are viewed probabilistically; by contrast, preschool children tend to view outcomes as definitely occurring or not (Inhelder & Piaget, 1958; Weisz, 1986a).

Grade-schoolers' concerns with power reflect their understanding of such abstract, potential causes as motivation (Rotenberg, 1980), effort, ability, task difficulty and chance (see Nicholls & Miller, 1984; Weisz, 1986a, for reviews). Although preschoolers can, after witnessing differences in performance, conclude that one child is more able than another (Morris & Nemeck, 1982), they lack grade-schoolers' conceptions of ability as relative capacity (i.e., as potential for success, relative to others). Grade-schoolers also have abstract notions of desire as predisposing outcomes, for example, by increasing the likelihood of efforts and by motivating actions that will influence desired outcomes (Aboud, 1985; Harter, 1982; Selman, 1980).

Control as freedom. As children enter adolescence they become more concerned with freedom (Gallatin & Adelson, 1970; Gallatin, 1972; Zellman & Sears, 1971). Freedom is the ability to take action and make decisions that are not contingent upon arbitrary forces. Prior to adolescence children are only dimly aware of larger systems, such as fate, societal institutions, and their own complex intrapsychic processes (e.g., personality, superego, instincts, and the unconscious), and the opportunities and constraints associated with these various systems.

The ability to make free choices requires more than an absence of restraints; it also requires an autonomous and consistent belief system. That is, coherent standards are needed to guide one's decisions and actions (Matza, 1964). Such standards are made possible by adolescents' increased self-consciousness and their formation of a complex and abstract psychological self—that is, an identity (Broughton, 1978; Erikson, 1968; Selman, 1980).

Regard for freedom of belief is seen in adolescents' (a) decreasing rote imitation of others' subjective beliefs (Rothbaum, 1979); (b) increasing tolerance of others who hold views differing from their own (Enright & Lapsley, 1981; Furth & McConville, 1981), and (c) increasing valuing of open-mindedness as a positive personality characteristic (Beech & Schoeppe, 1974).

Adolescents' investment in freedom of belief stems from their ability to reflect upon their abstractions (Damon & Hart, 1982; Elkind, 1974;

Piaget, 1967) and their ability to create higher order beliefs and belief systems (Selman, 1980).

SUMMARY

While mindful of the importance of cognitive deficit and delay, we emphasize the role of different levels of cognitive functioning in predisposing different types of problems. Whether cognitive functioning actually leads to problems depends upon a variety of noncognitive factors, such as stress and temperament. Our particular focus is on children's beliefs about and desire for control. Control is a pervasive but frequently ignored factor involved in psychological problems. In the preschool years children view control as magic, in middle childhood as power, and in adolescence as freedom. These developments in beliefs about control lead to corresponding changes in children's motivation and behavior.

NOTES

1. Throughout this book we use the term *psychological problems* rather than the term *psychopathology* to emphasize the continuity between "normal" functioning and extremely intense, persistent, and developmentally delayed functioning that is hurtful to the self and/or others. Labeling individuals as *psychopathological* sometimes serves to shroud psychological problems in a veil of mystery and obscure the individual's adaptive potential.

2. There is evidence of higher incidence of several internalizing behaviors, such as phobias and depression, in girls than in boys. By contrast, there is evidence of higher incidence of externalizing behaviors, particularly certain forms of rebellion, in boys than in girls. However, the findings depend upon the age ranges and the particular symptoms examined and are not fully consistent from study to study (Achenbach & Edelbrock, 1981; Rutter & Garmezy, 1983). Because of these complexities we do not treat this topic further.

3. Causality refers to that which occasions or effects a result, and intentionality refers to the determination to do a specified thing or to act in a particular manner.

4. The term *magic* was used by Piaget in a more restricted way than it is being used here. Our definition of magic is roughly equivalent to Piaget's definition of *nonnaturalistic causality,* the overarching construct of which magical thinking is a component.

2

A DEVELOPMENTAL MODEL OF PSYCHOLOGICAL PROBLEMS

THE FUNERAL: ILLUSTRATIONS OF COMMON PSYCHOLOGICAL PROBLEMS

The family gathering is large but subdued. Adults cluster in small groups, speaking warmly in hushed tones. They are pleased to be reunited, but sobered by the death of their beloved family member, Rachael. The children try to achieve some measure of control in this strange situation, and display quite different levels of cognitive maturity, and different psychological problems.

Edna and Ed: negativism and phobias. Rachael's sister, Martha, asks Edna, her 4-year-old daughter, to perform a social nicety: to say hello to a visitor. Edna ungraciously replies "No!," battle lines are drawn, and the conflict escalates when Edna refuses to sit quietly during a eulogy. Martha sees Edna as willful, stubborn and openly disobedient. However, Edna is concerned that her mother may control her, not in a rational sense of one person manipulating another, but in a magical sense. Just as fairy-tale characters can effect remote events through potions, wands, and abracadabras, Edna believes that her mother's instructions can magically dictate her course of action. In focusing on her mother's instructions, Edna fails to realize that she could exert a measure of control by *willingly* complying. Edna's defiance and her aggressive self-assertion are attempts to preserve her precarious sense of self-as-agent.

If only Edna were like her twin brother, Ed, Martha muses. Quietly, in the corner of the room, Ed is immersed in a make-believe play about Rachael's hospital room, where the theme is death. Later, the imaginary scene shifts to the cemetery, and the action centers on the ceremonial shoveling of dirt into the grave. Ed is frightened by what he has seen and heard as well as by his own fantastic imaginings about forces controlling death. Later that night he will refuse to go to bed, and he will be terrified by the dark. He has decided that he can ward off death if, and only if, he refuses to lie down. The ritualistic play and the magical rules give him control over his budding phobia.

Melanie and Mike: hostile aggression and inferiority. The 9-year-olds, Melanie, Mike, and a few other cousins, are huddled together in a corner of the same room, formulating a secret plan to cheer up Rachael's husband. Melanie is trying to control the group process by intimidating the others. Currently, she is focusing on Mike, whom she knows is self-conscious about his tearfulness. She smirks when he cries, and she ridicules him with a chant: "If you cry you will die." Her cruelty and bullying seem unprovoked to outsiders. But from Melanie's perspective, her attacks are fitting revenge for times that Mike has slighted her in the past. Melanie wants to hurt her cousin, both to settle old scores and to prove her superiority. Melanie has concerns and vulnerabilities that would never dawn on Edna and Ed. She is concerned about "looking bad" and being "humiliated" in front of her peers. To ward off these dangers, she adopts the philosophy: "The best defense is a good offense."

The victim of Melanie's assault, tearful, self-conscious Mike, realizes that he is not hiding his sadness about Rachael's death as well as his cousins are hiding theirs. Mike is just as concerned about his "standing" in the group as is Melanie. He is learning, however, that even in this "funeral group," his "place" is at the bottom of the hierarchy. Mike rarely initiates ideas because he knows they will be rejected or ridiculed. His preferred defense is to accommodate to situations because he lacks confidence in his ability to influence them. His other tactics are, in the long run, equally self-defeating: He tries to laugh when others mock him and he embraces the roles of scapegoat, laughing stock, and lackey. In fulfilling these roles he gains a degree of control over the humiliation and rejection that he sees as unavoidable.

Amy and Al: rebellion and depression. Rachael's 16-year-old daughter, Amy, stands toe-to-toe with her father, locking horns and exchanging verbal thrust and parry. At issue for the daughter are philosophical questions involving freedom. Although her father says she must, Amy refuses to greet mourners, "like some insincere Scarlett O'Hara" or to attend "the primitive ritual" of the burial at the cemetery.

Many of Amy's concerns are lofty and abstract in nature, involving the limitations of societally accepted institutions: family, religion, and cultural mores. Amy is rebelling because she sees her nonconformist ideas as central to her individual "identity." Were she to participate in the rituals it would amount to a "sham" and a "pretense" because she does not believe in them. Most of all, she is resisting others' attempts to control her thoughts and make her accept what she does not believe. In the finest tradition of her forebears, she is waging a revolution against the forces of tyranny—not simply for tangible gain, but for her inalienable rights.

Al, Amy's teenage brother, suffers equally throughout the funeral; but the flavor of his suffering is strikingly different. He has eaten little and has hardly slept for days. He speaks of feeling worthless, helpless, hopeless, and to some extent even responsible for Rachael's death. Here again, the plot involves the adolescent's "innermost self." He has been searching for "meaning" in the experience, but now concludes that the search is pointless in a world in which a loving mother could die in the prime of life; Al also feels that he must own and take responsibility for what he might have done to, or may once have thought about, Rachael. The depth of Al's depression is, ironically, a tribute to the complexity of his conception of control.

In the psychological hothouse of Rachael's funeral, six youngsters struggle to achieve a sense of control. In the process, six distinctive "styles" of psychological problems blossom—each shaped partly by general developments in children's understanding of control and partly by these youngsters' distinctive beliefs. The interplay of these forces is the focus of this book.

CONTROL AND PSYCHOLOGICAL PROBLEMS

Psychologists of diverse persuasions have posited connections between control beliefs and psychological problems. Included in this group are psychoanalysts, such as Adler (1964), who attributed many neurotic systems to disturbances in the will to power, and Erikson (1963), who linked a variety of emotional problems to frustration of the desires for autonomy, initiative, industry, and generativity. An emphasis on control beliefs is also evident in research on social learning theory. Rotter's (1966) external locus of control construct has been linked to psychological problems (see Lefcourt, 1976; Rothbaum, 1980) as has

Bandura's (1977, 1981) construct of self-efficacy. Other links between control beliefs and psychological problems are seen in Seligman's (1975) work on learned helplessness and Brehm and Brehm's (1982) work on psychological reactance. Control beliefs have been related to several specific forms of psychopathology, including externalizing problems, such as negativism (Wenar, 1982a; Brehm, 1981), hostile aggression (Wills, 1981), and rebellion (Brehm & Brehm, 1982; Fromm, 1941), and internalizing problems, such as phobias (Bandura, 1977, Gunnar-VonGnechten, 1978), inferiority (Dweck & Elliott, 1983; White, 1960), and depression (Seligman, 1975). To date, most of these relationships have been discussed without reference to developmental differences—in psychological problems or in beliefs about control.

Of the aforementioned theorists, White (1960, 1979) comes closest to articulating a developmental model linking control beliefs and psychological problems. White maintains that competence motivation undergoes repeated transformations through childhood, posing new challenges and crises at each stage of development. In early childhood he emphasizes the role of autonomy and self-will; in middle childhood, competition and rivalry; in adolescence, identity formation. A major difference between our position and White's is that White was not concerned primarily with the *cognitive developmental underpinnings* of developments in control motivation.[1]

There are many labels related to the control construct: agency, autonomy, causality, competence, contingency, effectance, efficacy, freedom, mastery, and power. These labels reflect substantive differences in the authors' theoretical orientations (see Weisz & Stipek, 1982, for a review of these differences).[2] Our definition of control—causal influence exerted in an intended direction—is a common denominator of several of the existing definitions.

HOW PSYCHOLOGICAL PROBLEMS WERE SELECTED

Because of an insularity of clinical and developmental literature, evidence documenting specific developmental changes in psychological problems is difficult to marshal (see Bobbitt & Keating, 1983; Ross, 1981; Wenar, 1984).

The main criterion used here in selecting psychological problems was that there be substantial evidence of developmental differences in the frequency of their occurrence. Some problems, such as enuresis, hyperactivity, and speech difficulties, which have been considered in previous reviews of developmental psychopathology, are not considered here, because they are now often thought to involve organic impairment. Also omitted are those rare problems thought to reflect severe and pervasive developmental deficits (e.g., autism, schizophrenia) and problems that are very situationally or behaviorally specific (e.g., night terrors, tics), or very situationally or behaviorally general (e.g., anxiety states, identity diffusion). Instead, we focused on problems at the midrange of the specificity-generality continuum because they strike an optimal balance between psychological meaningfulness (which is sacrificed if behavioral categories are too narrow) and reliability of assessment (which is sacrificed if categories are too broad; see Achenbach & Edelbrock, 1981; Zigler & Phillips, 1961). From the pool of problems so identified, we selected one of the internalizing type and one of the externalizing type at each age level.

CAUTIONARY NOTES

For heuristic reasons, we have depicted the two basic styles of psychological problems (i.e., internalizing and externalizing) and the three stages of development (i.e., early childhood, middle childhood, and adolescence) as neatly segregated. In reality, internalizing and externalizing behaviors are consistently intermingled, not only in the same child, but even in the same episode. For example, an adolescent with whom the first author worked in therapy used passivity and withdrawal as her primary means of dealing with her dread of social rejection and scholastic failure at school. She did not study at school or at home, she avoided social contact with her peers, and she tried to avoid going to school. Her manner of pursuing her goals, however, was often externalizing. She manipulated her parents by threatening aggression and by lying to them. An elementary school boy seen by the second author in therapy was anxious and withdrawn (internalizing) but also loud and hyperactive (externalizing) in school. At home, he was both depressed (internalizing) and disobedient (externalizing). Consistent with these examples, empirical studies reveal strong correlations between internalizing and externalizing scores for most groups of children (Achenbach & Edelbrock, 1983).

Similar qualifications regarding the developmental periods (i.e., the "ages" of magic, power, and freedom) are in order. First, the age ranges we mention are only rough approximations of truth. Our description of

2- to 6-year-olds, for example, may fit many but certainly not all 2- to 6-year-olds. Moreover, that same description may fit an immature school-aged child. It is interesting to note, however, that authors subscribing to quite different theories of child functioning have divided the developmental continuum in similar ways (see Noam, 1985, for a discussion of the concept of stages). Second, there is substantial development within, as well as between, each of the stages we describe. Early adolescents, for example, are likely to hold more idealistic and unrealistic notions about freedom than are late adolescents (see Piaget, 1967). Third, level of cognitive functioning, thus susceptibility to problems, often varies as a function of situation (see Rothbaum & Weisz, 1988). Rather than manifesting problems associated with a single stage in different circumstances and in different settings, children are likely to manifest problems associated with different stages (e.g., negativism at home, hostile aggression at school). Despite these qualifications, we believe that the links we draw between age ranges and psychological problems are useful.

NOTES

1. While White saw important links between cognition and control, he tended to view cognition as resulting from control motivation and as influencing the goals of control motivation (White, 1960, p. 25). By contrast, we emphasize the influence of cognitive development on the nature and expression of control motivation.

2. Deprivations in autonomy and freedom have been associated most often with externalizing problems (Brehm & Brehm, 1982; Wenar, 1982a), whereas deprivations in contingency, competence, and efficacy have been associated more with internalizing problems (Bandura, 1977, 1981; Rothbaum, 1980; Seligman, 1975; Weisz, Weiss, Wasserman, & Rintoul, 1987). Our own position emphasizes the distinction between primary control, efforts to change the world to make it fit one's own desires, and secondary control, attempts to change oneself to fit with the existing world (Rothbaum et al., 1982; Weisz, Rothbaum, & Blackburn, 1984; for related distinctions, see Lazarus & Launier, 1978; Rotter & Mulry, 1965). We argued that an exclusive reliance on primary control is likely to lead to externalizing behavior, and to suffering experienced primarily by others, whereas an exclusive reliance on secondary control is likely to lead to internalizing behavior, and to suffering experienced primarily by the self. Our emphasis in this book is more on developmental differences in control than on the aforementioned differences.

PART II

THE AGE OF MAGIC

3

PROBLEMS OF EARLY CHILDHOOD (2-6 YEARS): NEGATIVISM AND PHOBIAS

NEGATIVISM

In the movie *Kramer vs. Kramer,* five-year-old Billy gets ice cream from the freezer and starts to eat it, even as his father threateningly warns him not to do so. With attention riveted to his father, Billy slowly goes through each step of the forbidden sequence (opening the refrigerator, dishing out the ice cream, and so on). By the time he puts the first teaspoon in his mouth, it is clear that he is acting to win a battle. The ice cream may be attractive, but the gastronomical motive has faded into the background. The paramount issue is who will get his way.

Negativism, as defined by Wenar (1982a), is "intentional non-compliance to adult requests, directives, and prohibitions." Negativism can be physical (e.g., throwing an object), or verbal (e.g., the ubiquitous "no"), active (e.g., doing the opposite of what one was told to do), or passive (e.g., ignoring). Wenar identifies two basic types of negativism: "realistic negativism"—in which case the adult intrudes upon a strong ongoing interest and there is no comparable alternate activity, and "negativism for its own sake" (see Escalona, 1983), in which case it is "disproportionately intense and/or persistent in light of the (adult's) intrusiveness" (p. 6). The present review is also concerned with both types of negativism.

Wenar (1982a) conceptualizes negativism "in terms of that variable which has variously been labeled competence, autonomy, independence, mastery, or initiative" (p. 2). He downplays the distinctions among these constructs in order to emphasize their common basis: Children's efforts to counteract perceived intrusions upon their control. Wenar does not associate negativism with hostile aggression—behavior intended to injure or destroy—but with instrumental aggression—attempts to meet a personal need, most often a need "to maintain autonomy in the face of perceived threat" (p. 19).

Wenar amply documents his assertion that negativism flourishes between the second and fifth years of life. He reviews 21 findings— involving intelligence tests, mothers' reports, naturalistic observations and standard situations, using a variety of dependent measures. All but one of the findings substantiate this conclusion. Probably the most widely cited study is Macfarlane, Allen, and Honzik's (1954) investigation of mothers' reports of perverse negativism, habitual resistiveness, and the compulsive urge to do the opposite of what is expected or to do nothing at all. Incidence rose from 36% at 21 months to 65% at three years of age, and gradually fell thereafter. Heinstein (1969) obtained similar results: Between the ages of two and five, stubbornness was the most frequently reported psychological problem—more than 60% of mothers surveyed reported it. Disobedience also rose sharply at the age of two years and showed only a slight decline by the age of five.

Two studies not included in Wenar's review also indicate that negativism decreases from early to middle childhood. Patterson, Littman, and Brown (1968) found that when adults expressed agreement with 6- to 10-year-old children's preferences, many children opposed the adults by reversing their own initial preferences. This "negativistic" tendency declined with age. In another study, children whose freedom of choice was emphasized opposed an adult's attempt to influence their selection of a toy (Brehm, 1977). This oppositional behavior was evident for first graders but not for fifth graders. Brehm (1981) explains the findings from both of these studies in terms of "reactance," the tendency to react to a threat or loss of control by seeking to restore control.

Interestingly, compliance can sometimes be made palatable by giving it the aura of resistance and disobedience (see Brehm, 1981), as in this example involving the first author's son: From the time Abe was 2½ until he was 4½, it was useful to rely on a "Br'er Rabbit" strategy for inducing compliance. Abe's parents would tell him not to do the behavior they desired. In one variation of the game, Abe would ask his father to initiate the process—for example, "Daddy, tell me not to eat my peas." When his father obliged, Abe gobbled his peas. In essence this paradoxical strategy capitalized on the negativism of early childhood.

Levy (1972) reports a wide variety of manifestations of negativism in preschool children referred for therapy: "My cases include mutism, food refusal, bowel and bladder refusals (one patient, aged 27 months, said to me, 'I should move my bowels, but I won't'), oppositeness and inner negativism (asked to sit down, a 26-month-old boy stood up; asked to stand up, he sat down), . . . instances of pretending not to understand, and most frequently, as expressed by parents, 'Persisting in having his own way,' 'There's no way to make him obey,' and 'You can't talk him out of anything'" (p. 347). Another therapist (Moustakas, 1976) describes a four-year-old child who runs into the play room and goes immediately to a pail of water, shouting, "I'll throw it right on the floor! I'll put it right on the rug" and then proceeds to do so, exclaiming, "So there. So there"(p. 69). When the same child, 50 minutes later, is told she has only "a little longer today," she responds, "I won't go! . . . Not ever" (p. 72). Therapists' broad limits and their strategy of following the child's lead—cardinal rules of play therapy (Guerney, 1983, Moustakas, 1976)—can be seen as techniques tailored to the needs of the preschool oppositional child.

Not only is negativistic behavior common in an absolute sense, but it is common relative to other problems of this age. Johnson, Wahl, Martin and Johansson (1973) report that a full third of the behavior problems of preschool children involve noncompliance.

PHOBIAS

Phobias are fearful reactions that are disproportionately intense or persistent, given the objective threat of the stimulus objects or events. In many phobias the stimulus is ill-defined or benign. The phobic reactions can entail overt behavior, subjective feeling or thought, and/or physiological activity (Graziano, DeGiovanni, & Garcia, 1979).[1]

There is substantial evidence that phobias are prevalent in early childhood and that their incidence declines from early childhood through adolescence (e.g., Graziano et al., 1979; Morris & Kratochwill, 1983; Rutter & Garmezy, 1983).[2] The finding of a general decline is a robust one based on studies employing parent reports, teacher reports and direct observations, and using a variety of dependent measures (e.g., percentage of children experiencing at least one specific fear, mean number of fears, new cases). For example, Achenbach and Edelbrock (1981) report that more than 40% of randomly selected 4- to 5-year-old boys and girls experience fears of animals, places or situations other than school. The percentage drops to under 30% by 8 to 9 years. Similar figures have been reported by Jersild and Holmes (1935), Macfarlane et al. (1954), Marks (1977), and Morris and Kratochwill (1983). In a study employing data from interviews, test questionnaires and observations of 325 children and adults, Agras, Sylvester, and Oliveau (1969) found twice as many new cases of phobias in early childhood as in any other age period, and there was a rapid decline from ages 6 to 12.

The foregoing age trends apply to most types of fears. However, there are a few—involving noises, falling, strange objects, strange persons, and separations from caretakers—that are more prevalent in infancy than in early childhood. These fears rapidly decline during the preschool years (Rutter & Garmezy, 1983). The fears that have been found rather consistently to peak in incidence in early childhood involve specific places, objects, and events, most commonly animals, the dark, imaginary creatures, and nightmares (Angelino, Dollins, & Mech, 1956; Bauer, 1976; Jersild & Holmes, 1935; Lapouse & Monk, 1959; Maurer, 1965; Shepherd, Oppenheim, & Mitchell, 1971; Staley & O'Donnell, 1984). For school phobias and general fears (e.g., agoraphobia), especially those focused on social events, there does not seem to be a clear developmental progression (Angelino et al., 1956; Lapouse & Monk, 1959).[3]

One classic account of a phobia is Freud's (1963) case analysis that traces "Little Hans" from ages 3 to 5. Hans suffered from fear of being bitten by horses, and later fears of going out-of-doors and taking baths. Neither the boy nor his parents could explain his extreme anxiety, which persisted for several months despite repeated attempts to alleviate it. Though theorists of different persuasions interpret Hans's phobias differently, many agree that the horse and going outside were associated with other objects or events (e.g., separating from parents) that were the real source of anxiety (see Achenbach, 1982). As in many phobias, it was the child's difficulty linking the real source of anxiety to the manifest fear (e.g., horses) that gave the phobia its irrational quality.

One fear commonly reported in the clinical literature is fear of supernatural forces. For example, children may be afraid that "something" is under the bed and that it may grab their hand if they let it hang down. Sometimes childhood phobias involve faulty estimates of the likelihood of natural events. Achenbach (1982) describes the following example:

> Until Kirsten was 3½, she had slept in a room adjoining her parents' room. However, when her mother became pregnant for the second time, Kirsten's parents began to make plans to move Kirsten to an upstairs bedroom.

Shortly before the baby's birth, Kirsten began to express fears that the (exposed) roof beams (in her new bedroom) might break. . . . Kirsten's parents reassured her about the beams.

Just before the baby's birth, Kirsten was taken to her grandparents. She expressed fear that their house might break, although they had no exposed beams. (When) Kirsten came home from her grandparents . . . (she) was very reluctant to sleep, expressing fear of the beams.

Kirsten's beam phobia seemed to emerge as follows: Kirsten's anxiety was due to the arrival of a new sibling, the parents' rejection of her that this signified, the need to compete for parental attention. . . . Being alone upstairs in her room at night while the baby was . . . near her parents was the most specific focus of her fear.

Several months earlier, Kirsten heard (friends) jokingly describe how an exposed beam in their house had once cracked. . . . Thus, the frightening fact that exposed beams sometimes crack and that such beams existed in a setting already frightening to her . . . made the beams good candidates for becoming phobic objects. . . . Once the phobia had developed, it was reinforced by its success in earning Kirsten the privilege of sleeping near her parents.[4] (pp. 359-361)

Phobias are problematic in early childhood because of their intensity and frequency more than their duration. About half of childhood fears disappear in three months (Wenar, in press). It is possible that many instances of negativism are also quite transient. In explaining both of these early childhood problems, we will attempt to account for their termination, as well as their origins and maintenance.

SUMMARY

Preschoolers are especially susceptible to negativism and phobias. *Negativism,* defined as intentional noncompliance with adults' requests, directives, or prohibitions, can be physical or verbal and active or passive. Though frequently elicited by adults' intrusions, preschoolers' negativism is often more intense than the intrusion appears to warrant. *Phobias,* defined as fearful reactions that are more intense or persistent than the objective threat warrants, refers to behavior, feelings, thoughts, and physiological reactions. Fears of specific places, objects, events, the dark, imaginary creatures, and nightmares are the phobias most prevalent in early childhood. Although negativism and phobias are manifest in a sizable percentage of preschool children, episodes of these problems are usually short-lived.

NOTES

1. A variety of criteria have been used to distinguish between fears and phobias. These include intensity, maladaptiveness, persistence and age inappropriateness (Wenar, in press). Given the lack of consensus regarding how to operationalize the first three criteria, and the fact that the terms *phobias* and *extreme fears* are used inconsistently in the literature, we do not emphasize this distinction.

2. There is little evidence regarding the incidence of phobias in infancy. However, both behaviorists (e.g., Bandura, 1977) and analysts (e.g., Bornstein, 1949) emphasize the role of symbolic representation in phobias, and the capacity for symbolic representation increases dramatically from infancy to early childhood (Piaget, 1962).

3. The evidence regarding fear of school is difficult to interpret because younger children less often attend school and because school phobia typically involves other symptoms (Hersov & Berg, 1980; Rutter & Garmezy, 1983). The finding regarding generalized social fears suggests that it is fears of specific objects, places, and events, as opposed to more general fears that peak in incidence during early childhood. There are only a few specific fears—of snakes and storms—that do not decrease in incidence after early childhood, and even these generally first arise in early childhood (see Rutter & Garmezy, 1983). Graziano et al. (1979) and Morris & Kratochwill (1983) draw similar conclusions regarding the development of phobias.

4. Excerpt is from *Developmental Psychopathology* by Thomas M. Achenbach, © 1982, John Wiley & Sons, Inc. Reprinted by permission of John Wiley & Sons, Inc.

4

BELIEFS ABOUT CAUSALITY AND EARLY CHILDHOOD PROBLEMS

CAUSALITY IN EARLY CHILDHOOD: SALIENT AGENTS

Young children are notorious for believing in "obvious" but wrong causes. Sigmund Freud, in his case analysis of three-year-old "Little Hans," provides an example: In fishing for an explanation of why his sister cannot speak, Hans latches onto the only salient, related quality he has noted about her: "It's because she has no teeth." Another example involves the first author's four-year-old son who, when angered by his father not letting him touch the freshly painted walls, stomped away— toward his mother—and yelled at her, "I don't like your dress!" He evidently attributed his anger to the first salient object he noticed that displeased him.

The problem is that preschoolers understand that cause-effect relationships exist, as evidenced by their ubiquitous "Why?" but they do not understand how these relationships operate, as evidenced by the frequent inappropriateness of the query (Piaget & Inhelder, 1975). They fall prey to the belief in magical causes—salient objects and events that fortuitously capture their attention—because they are aware of and curious about causal questions that they are ill-equipped to answer.

Preschoolers' belief in magical control may, in large part, be due to their limited understanding of processes mediating between causes and outcomes. They often fail to use "causal chains" in explaining the contiguity between an initial action and its eventual outcome (Karniol, 1980). Thus if a child's arbitrary command (e.g., "Get me a bike for my birthday") leads to satisfaction of his or her desire, the child is likely to attribute magical control to the command and to ignore the intermediate sequence of events (see Fraiberg, 1959). Hand in hand with this limitation is an unreliable use of basic causal principles that are needed to ascertain objectively correct causes (see Sedlak & Kurtz, 1981, for a review). In particular, children have difficulty grasping the covariation of causes and effects—how often one event occurs in conjunction with and in the absence of another event. For example, a preschool child may well have difficulty considering the covariation between how she plays with a particular dog (roughly versus nicely), and whether the dog bites her or not. The child would, as a consequence, be likely to miss the essential cause-effect relationship operating in that situation. For children under age 7, adherence to this principle of covariation is "not entirely reliable even under ideal conditions and is easily undermined by a number of task complications" (Sedlak & Kurtz, 1981, p. 776; also see research on preschoolers' misunderstanding of contingency, reviewed by Weisz, 1986a).

Without firmly grounded causal principles, preschoolers are prone to perceive as causes those objects or events that are perceptually salient enough to capture their attention (Piaget, 1930; Dix & Herzberger, 1983; Sedlak & Kurtz, 1981). Before age 7, children are surprisingly willing to reject a subtle but perfectly covarying event as the cause, especially when an imperfectly covarying alternative is obviously similar to or temporally contiguous with the outcome and is attention grabbing. Continuing our earlier example, a child is likely to ignore the causal influence of teasing a dog in getting bitten—even though the events regularly occur together—if she instead focuses on an instance when the dog's yawning (and exposing its teeth) immediately precedes its biting her. By contrast, older children respect the rulelike character of causal relations and select only consistent covariates, even when contradictory cues vie for their attention (Dix & Hertzberger, 1983; Shultz & Ravinsky, 1977; Siegler, 1975; Weisz, 1986a).

Young children can comprehend covariation and other causal principles in simple, familiar, and nondistracting situations that pose few demands on attention and memory; but their frequent miscomprehension of these concepts in more complicated situations is a major contributor to the belief in magic (see Gruber & Voneche, 1977; Sedlak & Kurtz, 1981; Sharp, 1982; Weisz, 1981, 1983).

CAUSALITY AND NEGATIVISM

Preschoolers are prone to negativism when their personal desires, actions or physical presence are salient and they erroneously assume that the latter cause outcomes over which they exert no objective control. Piaget (1930) has provided considerable anecdotal evidence of young children's tendency to assume incorrectly that they have personal control. For example, Piaget (1930) asked, "Can the moon go where it likes, or is there something that makes it move along?" Until age 4 or 5, children tend to respond that their own movements force the moon to move along with them. Young children also believe that their own thoughts and mentioning of names can influence outcomes (Piaget, 1929).

More controlled laboratory and interview findings (Weisz, 1980, 1981; Weisz, Yeates, Robertson, & Beckham, 1982) have supported the view that young children assume that noncontingent events are controllable. For example, kindergarteners are much more likely than fourth graders to believe that factors like age, practice, and intelligence can influence outcomes in a totally chance-determined game (Weisz, 1980). In a variety of situations, preschoolers estimate their chances of success to be substantially greater than their prior experiences warrant (Morris & Nemeck, 1982; Nicholls, 1978; Parsons & Ruble, 1977; Rholes, Blackwell, Jordan, & Walters, 1980; Stipek, 1981, 1984). Whether this is owing to an inflated view of contingency between their actions and outcomes (see Piaget & Inhelder, 1975; Mischel, Zeiss, & Zeiss, 1974), to an inflated view of their general ability (Nicholls, 1978; Parsons & Ruble, 1977), to both (Weisz, 1986a; Weisz & Stipek, 1982), or to other cognitive distortions (Stipek, 1984), the end product is unjustified optimism. The preschool Oedipal child who suggests getting rid of daddy because he (the child) can "take care of" mommy, is a case in point. So too is the preschool child who believes that when she precedes a request with the word *please,* her request *has to be granted* (Berko Gleason, 1980).

A frequent consequence of the inflated expectancy of control is a vigorous reaction when control does not materialize. Unanticipated thwarting, or even threats of thwarting, can lead to active, sometimes aggressive "reactance": Attempts to overcome the thwarting and assert the control that had seemed so certain (Brehm, 1981). Bornstein's (1949) analysis of 5½-year-old Frankie illustrates this dynamic. The boy's feelings of "omnipotence" led him to give his parents nonsensical orders and to become greatly annoyed if they were not carried out. King Bobo, as Frankie called himself, went so far as to strike his parents for failing to obey his unspoken orders.

Reactance researchers maintain that a frequent but often overlooked factor in many frustrating encounters is loss of control per se, as opposed to loss of specific objects or privileges. Reactance research (Brehm & Brehm, 1982) demonstrates that if people expect control and then are deprived of it, they place increased value on the lost incentive. Conversely, if pressured to choose an initially favored incentive, they subsequently devalue it. The young child's tendency toward unrealistic control expectancies combined with the human susceptibility to reactance when expectations of control are thwarted, helps explain the pervasive negativism of early childhood. What the adult perceives as irrational opposition to directives may be the child's attempt to reassert personal control (Rothbaum, 1980).

There are, of course, many instances of negativism that may not involve either violated expectations or reactance. Rather, they may be simple assertions of will. Examples of the latter include a child who stands up when asked to sit down (Levy, 1972), and a child who gives seemingly automatic "no" responses to adult directives—even those the child wants to obey (Fraiberg, 1959). Such blatant opposition may often reflect young children's efforts to highlight their own causal influence. When children move to oppose prevailing currents, such as adults' directives or expectations, they heighten their own salience as causal agents. When children follow prevailing currents, their own causal influence is harder to detect.

One analysis of youngsters' assertion of self-will is offered by Fraiberg (1959):

> So the toddler, with only a few words at his command, has come upon "no" as a priceless addition to his vocabulary. He says "no" with splendid authority to almost any question addressed to him. Very often it is a "no" pronounced in the best of spirits and doesn't even signal an intention. It may even preface an opposite intention. He loves his bath. "Tony, would you like to have your bath now?" "No!" Cheerfully. (But he has already started to climb the stairs.) Marjorie can hardly wait to get outdoors in the morning. "Margie, shall we go 'bye' now?" "No!" (And she has started toward the door.) What is this? A confusion of meaning? Not at all. They know the meaning of "no" quite well. It's a political gesture, a matter of maintaining party differences while voting with the opposition on certain issues.

Thus negativism may reflect either violated expectations and reactance or efforts to assert personal agency. Common denominators of both phenomena are a focus on salient agents and a failure to recognize that most events are multiply determined (see Sedlak & Kurtz's, 1981, review of causal schemes).

CAUSALITY AND PHOBIAS

Like negativism, phobias involve a perception of contingency when none exists. Children are susceptible to phobias when they are impressed by a connection between an aversive outcome and temporally, spatially, or otherwise superficially related objects or events that they regard as causal. As mentioned earlier, 3½-year-old Kirsten may have attributed her fear of being separated from her parents to the first salient object that captured her attention—the beams. The beams were logical candidates because their visibility coincided with her fear, and because there were no obvious competing explanations for her fear. The beams were particularly likely to be seen as causes of her distress if she had reason to think they were dangerous (e.g., because of comments about cracked beams). Subsequent reassurances from her parents may have been ineffective because Kirsten had repeatedly experienced the connection between her strong fear and the presence of the beams.

As a result of their unreliable application of logical principles (e.g., covariation) in checking out their causal explanations, young children are prone to develop and cling to some very "irrational" fears. The common characteristic of the feared activity or object is that there is something perceptually (but not necessarily logically) compelling about its connection to the real aversive feelings and events. Also, it is something that children cannot control—except, perhaps, by avoidance. A child sent to an unsupportive day care setting may attribute his fear to a specific event or object associated with that setting, such as a food item, smell, or animal. The salience of these objects and the child's difficulty comprehending the true source of the fear, because of its abstract and psychological qualities, sets the stage for the development of the phobia.

Salient causality helps explain the transience as well as the tenacity of children's fears. They cling steadfastly to the fear—as long as their attention is captured by the connection between the feared object and the outcome. If circumstances or needs change, attention shifts, and the phobia can vanish as mysteriously as it emerged (see Wenar, 1987; Jersild & Holmes, 1935).

Preschoolers often fear supernatural forces because of their extreme salience and because their aversiveness resembles the aversive feelings the child is seeking to explain. Bauer (1976) found that 74% of kindergarteners are fearful of monsters, ghosts, or nightmares.

Little Hans again serves as an example—this time, of the role of salience in the causal reasoning associated with early childhood phobias. When this 3-year-old's anxiety (perhaps separation anxiety) was aroused by being taken out of the house for a walk, he tried to find an explanation for his negative feeling. Quite coincidentally, his attention focused on a horse (see Freud, 1963), an animal he had previously learned was capable of biting and stomping. The association of the anxiety with the potentially dangerous horse was too salient for him to ignore, both because he did not demand a logical explanation (e.g., in terms of mediating events) and because he did not comprehend the concept of coincidence (i.e., chance covariation). Thus he was firmly convinced he had found the cause of his anxiety (see Freud, 1963, p. 67). Moreover, his difficulty recognizing the existence of multiple causes (see Sedlak & Kurtz, 1981, for a review) made him unlikely to consider the possibility that other causes might be involved.

Like Little Hans, other preschoolers are especially likely to rely on evidence of salient similarity between events (in this case, between the experiencing of fear and a fear-arousing horse) in deciding whether they are causally related (Sedlak & Kurtz, 1981). Since causes are often similar in appearance to the outcomes they produce, similarity may often be a useful criterion in inferring causality. But during the age of magic, similarity is often treated as a sufficient criterion.[1]

The first author had an opportunity to work with a modern day Hans. Four-year-old Hanna had an irrational fear of motorcycles, lasting several weeks. Her parents recalled that it started on Halloween night, and that earlier in the day Hanna's baby sister was awakened by a loud motorcycle in the street. Hanna had mentioned this connection to her parents. Because of her intense sibling rivalry, Hanna dreaded all occasions when her sister was awakened and able to compete for her mother's attention. The awakening of the sibling was, therefore, a particularly aversive event. Later that night, when made fearful by the general ambience of Halloween and coincidentally observing a motorcycle in the street, Hanna quite naturally attributed her fear to the motorcycle. Having seized upon the salient (and wrong) cause, she was blind to other possibilities. The motorcycle phobia subsided markedly as Hanna's mother made more deliberate attempts to spend more time with Hanna.

Perception of contingency where it does not exist can contribute to phobias in other ways as well. According to Piaget, the young child tends to believe that rule violation will automatically lead to punishment, and often that personal suffering must be the result of some misdeed.[2] This illusory contingency may lead to "irrational" fear of retribution, and to irrational attributions of guilt or blame.

Erikson (1963) illustrates both phenomena with the example of Sam, a 4-year-old who was morbidly afraid of dying. Sam believed that he had caused his grandmother to die (of a heart attack) by roughhousing and thereby upsetting her after being told not to. Despite repeated reassurances from his parents that it was not his fault and that he would not die, Sam was convinced that he would be punished—by death—for what he had done. Similarly, Weiner and Graham (1984) found that adolescent children do not feel guilty about their grandparents' deaths, but younger children do. Younger children's vulnerability to guilt is often, we believe, owing to erroneous perceptions of contingency between their own prior misconduct and aversive outcomes.

SUMMARY

Preschoolers tend to assume that perceptually salient objects and events cause outcomes that those objects and events resemble, or that are proximate in time or space. Underlying this tendency is a general neglect of mediating events and a poor grasp of such basic causal principles as contingency and covariation. Inferring causality on the basis of salience sometimes leads children to overestimate their own control; this sets the stage for frustration and negativism when the anticipated control fails to materialize. Negativism may also help children detect their own causal influence; when they buck the tide their influence may be more salient than when they flow with the tide. At other times the child assumes that objects or events cause fear-eliciting outcomes because of the salience of the connection between the two. These mistaken causal inferences can lead to phobic avoidance of innocuous objects or events. The assumption that misdeeds lead to imminent justice can also provoke phobias.

NOTES

1. If children see themselves as resembling the fear-eliciting stimuli, they may be able to gain control over their fear (Freud, 1977). Afraid to cross the hall in the dark because of her dread of seeing ghosts, a young client of Anna Freud's hit upon a device that enabled her to do it: She would run across the hall making all sorts of peculiar gestures as she went. Triumphantly, she explained to her brother that there was no need to be afraid "as long as you pretend to be the ghost you might meet." As noted by Anna Freud, her "magic gestures represented movements that she imagined ghosts would make" (p. 111). This example has interesting therapeutic implications for working with preschool phobic children.

2. Karniol (1980) provides evidence that such misconceptions are, in large part, owing to young children's failure to concern themselves with mediating events, or "causal chains."

5

BELIEFS ABOUT INTENTIONALITY AND EARLY CHILDHOOD PROBLEMS

INTENTIONALITY IN EARLY CHILDHOOD: INTENTION-OUTCOME CONFUSION

Preschool children do not understand the psychological factors that are critical in determining the relationship between intentions and outcomes (Carroll & Steward, 1984; Selman, 1980). For example, children younger than 6 show little regard for the forseeability of outcomes (e.g., whether an actor knew his gun was loaded) in judging intent (Nelson-Le Gall, 1985; Shultz & Wells, 1985). Other psychological considerations relevant to intentionality—such as whether the behavior itself could possibly be unintended (e.g., bumping into someone could, punching could not), and whether it fits with the actor's customary disposition—also figure more prominently in the thinking of grade school than preschool children (Shultz & Wells, 1985).

In the absence of an adequate appreciation of the inner, psychological nature of intentionality, young children often confuse intent and outcome. This is seen in the tendency to infer intent from outcome. For example, young children often attribute malevolent intent to agents, including inanimate objects, simply on the basis of the aversive outcomes they cause (Piaget, 1929). A related phenomenon is children's tendency to ignore information about intent when it appears inconsistent with outcomes. Piaget (1948) reported that children up to the age of 6 evaluate an actor who commits more damage (i.e., breaks many cups) as naughtier than one who commits less damage (i.e., breaks one cup), even though the latter actor had worse intentions (i.e., he was engaged in purposefully disobedient behavior). Preschoolers are more influenced by the damage and less by the intentions than are older children.

In a review of research literature, Karniol (1978) found partial support for Piaget's claims: "Children at this stage (2-6 years old) do seem to depend on social consequences in their evaluations of behavior. However, . . . this dependence on social outcome information" would seem to be limited to well intentioned acts that result in damage" (p. 83; also see Keasey, 1977). That is, young children's evaluation of well intentioned actions is negatively biased by knowledge that the actions resulted in bad outcomes.

Besides inferring intent from outcome, young children infer outcome from intent. Piaget (1930) and later investigators have shown that preschoolers often assume that intentions can automatically lead to outcomes (see Nelson-Le Gall, 1985, for a review; also see Bettelheim, 1976). For example, Stipek (1984) found that young children had unrealistically high expectations for the performance outcomes of others when the children's reward was contingent upon good perfor- mance by those others. That is, when young children want others to do well they expect others to do well. There is also substantial evidence of a self-serving bias among preschoolers in judging their own performance (Stipek, 1984). When children intend to perform well, they later assume they have performed well. Finally, there is evidence that preschoolers sometimes assume that rules are closely tied to their own intentions. For older children, rules are more closely tied to underlying rationales involving reciprocity, merit and deservingness (Damon, 1977).

The close cognitive link between intentions and outcomes helps explain young children's failure to consider multiple intentions, espe- cially conflicting ones. In particular, they cannot understand the notion of ambivalence (Donaldson & Westerman, 1986). Thus, for example, they cannot reflect on wanting to be a big boy and go to the potty and wanting to avoid the potty to remain a baby. Preschoolers have difficulty understanding that intentions are intangible, psychological entities, and that they exist apart from the tangible outcomes with which they are concerned (Donaldson & Westerman, 1986).

One manifestation of children's failure to recognize their own mixed intentions is the sometimes bizarre intrusion of the unrecognized intention and its associated affect. For example, a child known to the first author, who was aware of his desire to use the potty but not of the conflicting desire to avoid it, alternated between sitting down and jumping up. In the process, he would say, "I uh wanna go pooh pooh," simultaneously expressing his dominant intention, "I *wanna* go pooh pooh," and his conflicting intention, "I *don't wanna* go pooh pooh." Similarly, when 3½-year-old Kirsten expressed her sibling rivalry by "handing the baby a toy with considerably more force than necessary" (Achenbach, 1982, p. 359), her aggressive intentions intruded into her dominant intentions to be loving and affectionate. Exclusive focus on a dominant intention, and failure to recognize intentions that ultimately interfere with its realization, leads to behavior that, from the child's perspective, appears to emerge out of nowhere. Such behavior is likely to fuel the belief in magical control.

Harter (1977) offers the following example of the young child's dilemma: "The young boy may staunchly insist that he only has feelings of love for his father. However, in the face of some upsetting punitive act on the part of the father, the child in a burst of emotion may blurt out, 'I hate you, I wish you were dead.' He may find that at this point in time, he can only experience . . . anger for his father. That is, he cannot simultaneously acknowledge both love and hate, he cannot conceptualize the temporary anger within the larger context of . . . an affective conceptual system, which (simultaneously) includes both positive and negative emotions. He has yet to achieve what metaphorically might be termed affective conservation—i.e., the recognition that particular events do not transform the entire emotional system, even though they may distort the balance of feelings temporarily" (p. 423).

There is empirical support for the foregoing claims. All 30 of the 4- to 5-year-olds in a study by Carroll and Steward (1984) saw multiple feelings as impossible. By contrast, 12 of the 30 8- to 9-year-olds saw multiple feelings as occurring either sequentially or simultaneously. Related findings are reported by Harter (1982) in her study of children aged 3 to 13: "The mean age at which children could give acceptable responses to the sequential occurrence of two emotions was between 6½ and 7½ years, and the average age by which children in this sample could conceptualize the simultaneity of two emotions was 9" (p. 40). Based on his research, Selman (1980, p. 38) draws a similar conclusion "(not until) about ages 7 to 12, . . . (are) persons' thoughts or feelings seen as potentially multiple, for example, curious, frightened, and happy."

INTENTIONALITY AND NEGATIVISM

The tendency to automatically connect intention and outcome makes the 2- to 6-year-old prone to negativism. Children at this age expect control simply on the basis of their desire for control. If their expectations are thwarted, which is a common occurrence since their expectations are so often unrealistic, they manifest reactance—enhanced effort, anger, and aggression directed toward gaining the lost control. A 4-year-old, whose father enters the room when he is cuddling with his mommy, says, "Go away, Daddy!" and fully expects his command to be acted upon. Another child, who regretted biting off all the toes of her doll, insisted that the toes were still there. When the intention is a strong one, even older preschoolers manifest this tendency: The first author's 6-year-old son protested that he *could* go to the beach because it was *not* raining, despite his parents repeated reminders that it was *pouring*. Negativism, then, results from preschoolers' tendencies to (a) believe that the world will conform to their intentions, (b) deny realities that conflict with their intentions, and (c) strenuously resist adults' attempts to "set them straight."

Preschool children also mistakenly assume connections between their intentions and rules. They are invested in rules, but only as long as rules work in their favor. This predisposes them to impudent disregard of authority and convention, in favor of "rules" they have invented to suit their momentary needs (Damon, 1977).

Interestingly, Kuczynski, Radke-Yarrow, and Kochanska (1985) found that the negativism of 3-year-olds, as compared to 2-year-olds, more often takes the form of asking for a reason for parental directives or giving a reason for disobeying them. These responses may reflect a greater awareness of and investment in rules by preschoolers than by toddlers (Damon, 1977). But preschool children are unlikely to consider reasons for rules when the reasons are independent of their own intentions. Thus they ignore the competence of the adult or the fact that adults take care of children—reasons that legitimize authority in the eyes of children older than 7 years. Moreover, they are prone to see themselves as not having to obey rules they do not want to obey (Damon, 1977). Based on his extensive research on moral judgment in early and middle childhood, Damon (1977, p. 246) concludes that preschoolers regard rules as "momentary regularities that may be followed or ignored at will."

Many situations that elicit negativism also elicit the desire to conform (Brehm, 1981). For example, a parental directive is likely to elicit a desire to please the adult, to depend on the adult's judgment, or to avoid punishment—as well as a desire for reactance. Young children's neglect of the former motives when the latter motive is salient is probably often owing to their difficulty in contemplating more than one intention at a time. Research has shown that when young children spontaneously experience one intention (e.g., to engage in wrongdoing), they generally cannot formulate strategies for expressing contrary intentions (Carroll & Steward, 1984).

As he refuses to eat his peas, the young child is unlikely to also contemplate his fear of adult disapproval; in fact, the preschooler's tendency to infer his intent from his actions is likely to lead to increased awareness of his or her intentions not to comply. Older children's ability to recognize conflicting intentions can lead to a tempering of their reactance.[1]

INTENTIONALITY AND PHOBIAS

Primitive understanding of intentionality can set the stage for phobias as well as for negativism. A salient aversive agent that is temporally, spatially or otherwise associated with an aversive outcome may well be perceived by the preschool child as intentionally causing the aversive outcome. As a consequence, the child may develop unrealistic fears of the recurrence of the dreaded event perpetrated by one with seemingly malicious intent. An aggressor who intends to harm us is far more sinister and is more likely to repeat his harmful actions than one who accidently inflicts harm.

In cases in which an agent associated with hurt appears to have both positive and negative intentions toward the self, the preschool child's attention is likely to be captured by negative intentions because they are congruent with hurtful outcomes. For example, when a parent scolds a child for misbehaving, the child is likely to focus on the parent's intent to inflict hurt rather than the intent to help alter the child's behavior. Preschool children's pervasive difficulty in perceiving conflicting intentions makes it difficult to reassure themselves that sometimes, or in some respects, the aggressor does not intend to inflict hurt. Rather, the agent is likely to be seen as all bad, and the bad agent is dissociated from any of its good characteristics (see the psychoanalytic notion of "splitting," Kegan, 1982; Kris, 1984). Malicious monsters, witches, and other fairy-tale characters may be popular in early childhood in part because they sharply differentiate between forces of good and evil (see Bettelheim, 1976).

Preschoolers' difficulty in recognizing conflicting intentions may lead them to disown their own unacceptable intentions. Consistent with this speculation are findings that preschoolers deny negative emotions and self-attributes (Glasberg & Aboud, 1982; Harter & Buddin, 1987; Stipek, 1981a). In cases in which unacceptable intentions are too strong to completely deny, preschoolers may acknowledge their existence but project (i.e., attribute) them onto external forces (Bettelheim, 1976). After doing so, children quite naturally develop fears of these forces; they are seen not only as malicious, but as out of their control. For example, in toilet training, the child's socially sanctioned intention to achieve success is often more salient than the socially disapproved-of intention to impulsively let go, even when the latter intention is acted upon. Illustrating this dynamic is the following remark of a four-year-old who awoke to a wet bed: "It rained in my bed last night." A concern that the mysterious malicious force may again do its dirty work can then lead to a fear of going to sleep.

Similarly, Steinhauer and Berman (1977) cite the case of a 4½-year-old who feared that her mother would die because the child had projected her own anger at her mother (because of the mother's seeking a divorce) onto an imagined evil character. Her projection resulted from her inability to coordinate her positive and negative feelings toward her mother. She did not perceive her projected unacceptable intentions as within her control and became fearful that the external agent would harm her mother.[2]

The preschool child's unacceptable intentions can contribute to phobic reactions even when these intentions are not projected outside the self. Preschoolers' tendency to equate evil wish with evil deed can lead them to fear retribution for their harmless fantasies. For example, Little Hans expected to be drowned in the bath by his parents as punishment for his wishes that his younger sister would drown while bathing.

SUMMARY

Preschool children have little understanding of the processes mediating between intention and outcome, and they have difficulty recognizing the existence of conflicting intentions. They sometimes assume that their intentions will automatically lead to desired outcomes; when the outcomes do not materialize the children manifest reactance. Preschoolers' limited grasp of the rationales underlying rules makes them susceptible to the belief that rules can be made and altered to serve the self's whims. Moreover, they have difficulty tempering reactance because of their limited ability to entertain nonsalient intentions (e.g., to avoid punishment and to please adults) that are in conflict with reactance. The tendency of preschoolers to attribute aversive outcomes to others' negative intent leads to excessive fear of the other and fear of repetition of the outcome. Similarly, when children project their own socially unacceptable desires onto the external world, they experience those desires as externally controlled and as potentially harmful to themselves. When they are aware of their own unacceptable desires, children are susceptible to a fear of retribution, again because of confusion between intention and outcome.

NOTE

1. Just as extreme reactance makes it difficult for the child to consider competing motives to comply (e.g., to please the adult), extreme motivation to comply makes it difficult for the child to consider competing motives for reactance. There is evidence that young children are especially likely to comply with adult directives (Minton, Kagan, & Levine, 1971), to conform to parental wishes regarding morality (Damon, 1977; Kohlberg, 1969; Piaget, 1948; Rawls, 1971), and to imitate a model's salient behavior (Bandura & Huston, 1961; Yando, Seitz, & Zigler, 1978).

PART III

THE AGE OF POWER

6

PROBLEMS OF MIDDLE CHILDHOOD (6-13 YEARS): HOSTILE AGGRESSION AND INFERIORITY

HOSTILE AGGRESSION

Hostile aggression is defined as malevolent verbal or behavioral assaults motivated by a desire to gain status or self-esteem, to demonstrate one-upmanship, or to retaliate against perceived threats to or deprivations of these gains. Methods include bullying, teasing, insulting, and humiliating or otherwise derogating others; the common element is ego assaulting so as to reduce others' self-esteem or sense of well-being. Hostile aggression is distinguished from instrumental aggression, which is focused on obtaining objects, privileges, or territory, and from impulsive aggressive outbursts.

The hostile-instrumental distinction was first articulated by Feshbach (1970) and later elaborated upon by Hartup (1974, 1983). Hartup reports an increase in what he variously terms "person-oriented aggression," "ego assaults" and "hostile aggression" from preschool (ages 4-6) to the early grade school years (ages 6-7). While the 6- to 7-year-olds showed less overall aggression, a significantly higher percentage of their aggression was classified as hostile. For example, in response to derogation, the older children produced "some type of insult or reciprocated threat to the self-esteem" 78% of the time, whereas younger children did so only 53% of the time. By contrast, instrumental aggression—that is, aggression aimed at gaining or retrieving an object, territory, or privilege—showed a decrease with age. McCabe and Lipscomb (in press) also found that the proportion of verbal aggression that is hostile as opposed to instrumental increases over the grade school years.

Sullivan (1953), a widely cited authority on problems in middle childhood, claims that there is a heightened incidence of "malevolence" during the "juvenile" and "preadolescent" periods (ages 6-12). Sullivan emphasizes children's "hatred," their reluctance to show tenderness or cooperation, their perception of themselves as unloved and as living among enemies, and a competitive desire to "put others down." This description of malevolence is similar to the present description of hostile aggression.

Clinical observations of increased bullying and derogation of others during the school years have been noted by others (e.g., Allport, 1961). Drawing on various anthropological findings, Fine (1981) notes that "preadolescents have an international reputation for being candid about their feeling toward disliked others." Based on his own three-year field observation study, Fine emphasizes the ego-enhancing and status-elevating effects of assaulting others' egos:

> It is a frequent observation that preadolescents can be distressingly cruel to each other, but the social context of this cruelty is not sufficiently emphasized. The cruelty is almost always expressed in the presence of friends. Insults seem to be expressed as much for reasons of self-presentation to one's peers as to attack the target. (p. 46)

Fine offers the following example:

> Hardy sees Tommy get on the bus and announces loudly, "Tommy sucks." Rod adds: "Tommy's a wuss." In unison, Jerry and Rod tell Tommy as he approaches, "You suck." Rod, particularly, is angry at Tommy. "Harmon can't play because of you. What a fag!" Tommy doesn't respond to the abuse from his older tormentors, but looks dejected and perhaps near tears (which is what Rod and Hardy later tell Harmon). The insults build in stridency and anger as Hardy calls Tommy a "woman." Jerry knocks off [Tommy's] hat, and Rod says, "Give him the faggot award." Finally, Jerry takes the baseball cap of Tommy's friend and seatmate and tosses it out the window of the moving bus. (p. 46)

Empirical support for the claims of Sullivan and Fine comes from Karniol's (1985) findings of an increase in derogation of unfortunate others from kindergarten to the late elementary school years. Research on competitive behavior also supports the claim that behavior intended to put others down increases in middle childhood: Kagan and Madsen (1976) found an increase from age 5-6 to 8-10 in a sample of Mexican and American children (there were no differences between the 2- to 5-and 5- to 8-year-olds); McClintock, Moscowitz, and McClintock (1977) found an increase from age 3½ to 7; and Toda, Shinotsuka, McClintock, and Stech (1978) found an increase from the second to the sixth grade for children from four cultures. These authors claim that although competition as a means of maximizing gains begins around 4½, competition does not function as an "autonomous" motive (i.e., an end in its own right, rather than for instrumental gain) until approximately age 7 (Knight, Dubro, & Chao, 1985). The contests (e.g., staring) and competitive activities (e.g., board games) of children this age (Higgins & Parsons, 1983) are examples of grade-schoolers' noninstrumental competitive behavior.

We have found only one study showing changes in the amount of competitiveness from middle childhood to adolescence. Based on parental reports, Macfarlane et al. (1954) report a steady decline in "excessive competitiveness" from the youngest ages examined, 7-8, to the oldest ages examined, 13-14.

The developmental change occurring from middle childhood to adolescence appears to affect the nature rather than the amount of competition. Berndt (1982) found that eighth graders, as compared to sixth graders, were more reluctant to engage in competition with friends, but were no more reluctant to compete with unfamiliar others. Other authors have found more competition in interactions with friends than with acquaintances in the grade school years (Fine, 1980; 1981; Staub & Noerenberg, 1981). A related finding is that there is an emphasis in adolescence on intergroup, as opposed to intragroup, rivalry and aggressive competition (Schwendinger & Schwendinger, 1985)—evidently reflecting a shift away from competition with close associates. In middle childhood hostile aggression often occurs within the group, and former friends are common targets (Fine, 1981).

Studies that have examined the overall incidence of meanness, cruelty, and bullying in middle childhood and adolescence do not show clear-cut age-related differences (Achenbach & Edelbrock, 1981; Olweus, 1988), but these studies have not distinguished between aggression against close associates and aggression against more distant acquaintances.

Findings from large-scale surveys of aggression in childhood, while obviously relevant to the present discussion, are difficult to interpret because of the failure to distinguish between instrumental and hostile forms of aggression. Almost all of these studies indicate a decline in incidence of overall aggression from the earliest ages studied (typically 4-6) through the latest ages (typically 14-18; see Achenbach & Edelbrock, 1981; Griffiths, 1952; Loeber, 1982; Patterson, 1982; Rutter & Garmezy, 1983). Since instrumental aggression appears to be considerably more prevalent in early childhood than in middle childhood (see Hartup, 1974), these findings tell us little about the developmental course of hostile aggression. When types of aggression are attended to, different developmental patterns may emerge. For example, in their cross-cultural study, Whiting and Whiting (1975) found a decrease in frequency of physical assaults but an increase in insults (a form of hostile aggression) from ages 3-5 and 6-8.

Our conclusion from the foregoing strands of developmental evidence—that there is a peak in incidence of hostile aggression in middle childhood—is echoed in prominent reviews of the literature. For example, Wenar (1982b) maintains that

> after the preschool period, aggression in the form of crude physical attack in reaction to the immediate situation declines, and children's behavior becomes progressively more intentional, retaliatory and symbolic. Children are concerned with getting even and paying back in kind, while their aggressive repertoire proliferates: bickering, quarreling, teasing and swearing abound, along with bullying, prejudice and cruelty. (pp. 61-62)

A similar conclusion is drawn by Maccoby (1980):

> After the preschool years, aggression changes qualitatively: it is less often a struggle over objects and more often a clash of egos. Insults (that is, ego attacks) become both a major means of hurting others and a major occasion for retaliation.... Children become much more sophisticated in judging when others have intended to hurt (and hence, when retaliation is justified) and how to hurt their chosen victims. (pp. 157-158)

This last point, regarding the role of perceived intent, will be emphasized later.

INFERIORITY

Inferiority is defined as a self-perception that one is lower in status, or less capable than others, physically, intellectually, or socially. Behaviorally, inferiority is manifested in negative self-evaluations, anxiety,[1] and self-defeating behaviors, such as extreme passivity and withdrawal, task-inappropriate behavior and acting the role of the scapegoat. By engaging in these behaviors, children inadvertently increase the likelihood that they will experience defeat and victimization. Victimization is commonly experienced by unpopular children—that is, children who occupy inferior status in the social hierarchy.

There is considerable evidence that preschoolers have extremely high and unrealistic performance expectations and rankings of their own ability relative to others (Nicholls, 1979a; Stipek, 1981a). Their high expectations persist even in the face of repeated failure (Parsons & Ruble, 1977; Stipek, 1981b). The trend toward lower self-evaluation continues through the early grade school years (i.e., up until approximately age 9)—a developmental pattern observed both in cognitive domains and social domains (see Weisz, 1986a, for a review). There is also evidence of an increase from the preschool to the grade school years in children's tendency to blame themselves unfairly for aversive outcomes, such as the death of a loved one or a parental divorce (e.g., Wahl, 1958; Wallerstein & Kelly, 1980), but this evidence is largely anecdotal.

A less clear developmental pattern emerges when one examines the shift in self-esteem from middle childhood to adolescence. Most studies do not indicate significant age differences (see Wylie, 1979, for a review; also see Harter, 1982). However, Achenbach and Edelbrock (1981) did obtain a clear-cut developmental effect: Parents rated their children as experiencing more feelings of worthlessness and inferiority in middle childhood than in either early childhood or adolescence.

Rosenberg's (1979) findings suggest that, as children enter adolescence, there is a shift in the targets rather than the degree of negative self-esteem. In middle childhood (ages 8-11), 24.5% of children identify physical characteristics and 55% identify abilities and activities as their chief point of shame; the corresponding figures for adolescents (age 14 and over) are 12.5% and 42.5%. By contrast, adolescents are more likely to identify traits like self-control as points of shame than are grade school children (percentages for the two age groups are 32.5 and 14.5, respectively). Thus it is not that grade school children feel worse about themselves than do adolescents, but they feel worse about different things.[2] *Inferiority* seems an apt term for the self-esteem problems of middle childhood, which involve fairly external characteristics and skills that can be relatively neatly ordered along a linear hierarchy.

An example of inferiority relevant to a specific skill is provided by Anna Freud (1977, p. 100):

A girl of ten went to her first dance, full of delightful anticipation. She fancied herself in her new frock and shoes, upon which she had expended much thought, and she fell in love at first sight with the handsomest . . . boy at the party . . . She made advances to him but . . . when they were dancing together, he teased her about her clumsiness. This disappointment was at once a shock and a humiliation. From that time on she avoided parties and lost her interest in dress and would take no trouble to learn to dance.

This anecdotal evidence is paralleled by empirical findings: According to Achenbach and Edelbrock (1981), parents indicate an increased incidence in middle childhood of both "not liked by other children" and "gets teased." Moreover, there is evidence of a link between unpopularity and low self-esteem in middle childhood (for reviews, see Hartup, 1974, 1983; see also Lefkowitz & Tesiny, 1985).[3] Low social-status grade school children attribute negative interpersonal outcomes to internal factors, and positive outcomes to external factors more than do high social-status children (Ames, Ames, & Garrison, 1977). Wylie (1979) notes that the relationship between low socioeconomic status and low self-regard is stronger in those studies employing adults. Several authors have implicated peer rejection in the self-esteem problems of grade school children (Erikson, 1963; Hartup, 1983; Poznanski, 1982; Sullivan, 1953).

Evidence that grade school children who have inferior social status may inadvertently invite the abuse heaped on them is provided by Putallaz and Gottman (1981). These authors found that "unpopular" children were particularly likely to disagree with and criticize their peers and to fail to provide either a general reason or rule for their disagreement or a constructive alternative. Moreover, they relied on group entry techniques that maximized the likelihood they would be responded to in an ignoring or rejecting manner by their peers.

Similar findings were obtained by Dodge, Schlundt, Schocken, and Delugach (1983). Children who were rejected by their peers exhibited behavior that appears to invite rejection: They showed few group-oriented statements or attempts to become integrated into the group by imitating others, and numerous disruptive and attention-getting behaviors. Other studies (Dodge, 1983; Coie & Kupersmidt, 1983) support the conclusion that unpopular children invite abuse by acting inappropriately and by failing to contribute positively to group process.

The notion that many grade-schoolers participate in their victimization is echoed by Sullivan (1953, p. 232), who describes "people [who] are willing to yield almost anything, as long as they have peace and quiet," and by Olweus (1978) who describes the whipping boys in his research as "unwilling or unable to ward off attacks even by fairly harmless antagonists" (p. 142). In a later report, Olweus found that the percentage of children who are frequent targets of aggression decreases dramatically from middle childhood to adolescence (Olweus, 1988). We will attempt to show how the high incidence of self-defeating behaviors during this age period reflects, at least in part, grade-schoolers' acute awareness of and desire for power, and their perception that power is difficult to obtain.

Extreme passivity and withdrawal (e.g., giving up on solvable problems) and task inappropriate behaviors (e.g., glancing away from the task at hand while problem-solving) are also associated with inferiority (see Chapter 7, this volume). These behaviors increase from the preschool to the grade school years (Boggiano & Ruble, 1979; Rholes et al., 1980; Weisz, 1986a; Dweck & Elliott, 1983). Preschoolers manifest these behaviors only in situations in which failure and uncontrollability of outcomes is made extremely salient, and even then, the underlying dynamic is unlikely to be feelings of relative inferiority (Dweck & Elliott, 1983).

SUMMARY

Grade school children are especially susceptible to hostile aggression and inferiority. *Hostile aggression,* defined as malevolent assaults intended to increase status, self-esteem or one-upmanship, or to retaliate against losses of these goals, includes behavioral and verbal attacks against others' egos. Relative to instrumental aggression, which is focused on more tangible gain, hostile aggression increases from early to middle childhood. Although hostile aggression is also prevalent in adolescence, adolescents are probably less likely to direct their hostility against close associates. *Inferiority,* defined as a perception of self as low in status or capability, is manifest in negative self-evaluations and self-defeating behavior (victimization). Negative self-evaluations increase from early to middle childhood. From middle childhood to adolescence the targets of negative evaluations shift from specific skills to general traits. Problems involving unpopularity, which peak in middle childhood, often reflect low self-esteem and the perception that self can gain control only by playing the role of the victim.

NOTES

1. Measures of anxiety in middle childhood entail many items assessing low self-esteem, and the two constructs are largely overlapping (Nicholls, 1976b).

2. They also feel better about different things: As the first author's 7-year-old said the day he learned to whistle: "Now I can whistle, tie my shoes, and snap my fingers—I can do everything."

3. By contrast, there is considerable controversy regarding the link between unpopularity and aggression. Dodge (1983) has found a connection between the two, but several other investigators have not found that unpopularity relates to aggression (e.g., Feshbach, 1970; Olweus, 1978). Staub (1979) reports that it is the targets of aggression more so than the perpetrators who are unpopular. In this book we do not assume that aggression and unpopularity are related.

7

BELIEFS ABOUT CAUSALITY AND MIDDLE CHILDHOOD PROBLEMS

CAUSALITY IN MIDDLE CHILDHOOD: POTENTIAL AGENTS

As noted in Chapter 4, preschoolers assume that objects and events have causal influence largely on the basis of their concreteness and salience. By middle childhood, it is not always the concrete, salient agent that is credited with the most causal influence; after the age of 7-8, the role of covert influences is frequently mentioned (e.g., Feldman & Ruble, 1981; Livesley & Bromley, 1973; Shantz, 1975). The flavor of this process is depicted in the novel *Lord of the Flies* (Golding, 1959). There the bully Jack initially strives to become the most dominant figure in a group of shipwrecked grade school boys by literally singing his own praises: "(I should be the leader) because I can reach high c." But the peer group bestows the mantle of leadership and power on Ralph instead, largely on the basis of more abstract qualities, such as intelligence and interpersonal sensitivity.

Corresponding to the shift from concrete causes to abstract causes is a shift from causal agents that have *immediate* influence to those that have the *potential* to influence outcomes. The causal constructs that are relied upon in middle childhood—including ability (e.g., Nicholls & Miller, 1984; Rholes & Ruble, 1984; Nicholls, 1978), effort (e.g., Nicholls, 1978; Nicholls & Miller, 1984), task difficulty (e.g., Nicholls & Miller, 1983), and chance (e.g., Nicholls & Miller, 1985; Weisz et al., 1982)—all hinge on an understanding of potential. Preschoolers rarely invoke these constructs in logically appropriate ways.

In the preschool years, ability is understood only in terms of immediate and absolute outcomes, such as completing all the pieces of a puzzle (e.g., Nicholls & Miller, 1984; Rholes & Ruble, 1984). By contrast, in middle childhood ability is understood in terms of prior and relative outcomes and their potential implications. For example, a history of completing puzzles faster than most children do suggests a similar outcome in future trials. Preschool children have more difficulty than do grade school children with making inferences regarding relative ability even when information regarding prior behavior and outcomes is very simple and clearly presented (e.g., Boggiano & Ruble, 1979; Morris & Nemeck, 1982; Heller & Berndt, 1981; see Ruble, 1983, for a review). For example, older children (9- to 10-year-olds) can predict how an actor will behave based on traits or abilities revealed in that actor's prior behavior. By contrast, younger children (5- to 6-year-olds) do not predict consistency across situations even when they are helped to label the actors' behaviors with appropriate trait or ability terms (Rholes & Ruble, 1984).

Preschool children seemingly do not regard dispositional factors as stable, abiding characteristics; consequently, they are less likely to see behavior as rulelike and predictable (Heckhausen, 1981; Ruble, 1983). They also do not use stable dispositional constructs in their descriptions of others (e.g., Barenboim, 1981; Livesley & Bromley, 1973; Peevers & Secord, 1973; Rotenberg, 1982). Frey and Ruble (1985) found that only 20% of kindergartners but 61% of fourth graders referred to general ability in explaining an actor's behavior. Younger children's attention seems to be focused on an actor's immediately preceding behavior and outcomes. This focus goes hand in hand with their difficulty recognizing dispositions (Flavell, 1977; Nicholls, in press; Ruble, 1983).

An appreciation of stable characteristics is evident in Tarkington's (1923) story about nine-year-old Lawrence Coy who misbehaves at his birthday party. Later that evening, Lawrence balks at reciting one line from his prayers: "I know that I have a character and I know that I am a soul." Lawrence's hesitation suggests that he is concerned about more than his momentary misbehavior, and is focused instead on the implications of this misbehavior for that stable aspect of self known as character.

The understanding of stable psychological constructs precedes the ability to draw comparisons among constructs (Barenboim, 1981). Not surprisingly, then, preschool children have not been found to rely on social comparison processes in making self-evaluations of abstract characteristics (Ruble, 1983). Children before age 7 years use feedback regarding the performance of other children only when the comparisons are highly salient and when they are judging very concrete outcomes, such as running speed (Morris & Nemeck, 1982; Ruble, 1983). Even then they fail to compare rates of progress (Frey & Ruble, 1985). In other situations they infer evaluations almost exclusively on absolute performance standards (e.g., completion of a puzzle) or on the actor's immediately preceding success or failure (see Ruble, 1983; Dweck & Elliott, 1983; and Rholes & Ruble, 1984, for reviews). Young children fail to use social comparison information even when absolute standards are ambiguous and when they are given rewards for accuracy (Ruble, 1983).

Grade school children have an enhanced understanding of ability in part because they come to conceive of it in relation to other abstract causes, such as task difficulty. For example, about 30% of 5- to 6-year-olds, but 70% of 7- to 8-year-olds, and 97% of 9- to 10-year-olds realize that smartness is *best* measured by success at tasks that the fewest others could do—as opposed to by success at tasks that most others could do (Nicholls, 1978). That is, grade-schoolers realize that more difficult tasks require more ability (see Aboud, 1985; Nicholls & Miller, 1984). Grade school children also have a better understanding of the relationship between an actor's ability, effort, and chance. The first author's 7-year-old aptly summarized the role of ability in chance-determined and skill-determined games as follows: "No one can ever be a really good player at Candyland, but someone can be a really good chess player" (see Weisz, 1980, 1981).

Unlike adolescents, however, grade school children are *not* systematic in their consideration of the interdependence of the causal factors mentioned here. Moreover, their understanding of each of these factors is not as complex as it is in adolescence. For example, grade school children conclude that students who gain equal scores after unequal effort are equally bright. In other words, "the implications [of their understanding of ability] are not systematically followed through" (Nicholls & Miller, 1984, pp. 196-197). Similarly, even when grade school children identify a task as chance determined, they are still likely to predict better outcomes for "smart" kids than for "not very smart" ones, and for kids who try hard as compared to those who do not (Weisz et al., 1982). As we shall see next, both the advances and the limitations in grade-schoolers' understanding of causal factors help account for the psychological problems of this age period.

CAUSALITY AND HOSTILE AGGRESSION

As children recognize that they have stable abilities and that the evaluation of these abilities depends upon the self's standing relative to others, there is an increased likelihood of hostile aggression. According to Wills (1981), persons can enhance their subjective well-being through comparison with a less fortunate other (see Brickman & Bulman, 1977; Sullivan, 1953). This "downward comparison" is often achieved through "scapegoating" and "hostile aggression." Causing the other person harm creates the opportunity for comparison with a less fortunate other.

Wills reviews evidence that downward comparison is often triggered by the experience of ego threat. Ego threat, in turn, is most likely when comparisons are made between dispositions. Since preschoolers are not likely to focus on dispositions when comparing themselves to others, hostile aggression is unlikely to occur prior to middle childhood.

Wills's social comparison theory provides a compelling explanation of retaliatory behavior: The experience of being put down leads to hostile aggressive efforts to reestablish one's standing vis-à-vis the person who has gained the upper hand. Wills's theory is also well suited to explain displacement of aggression and derogation of innocent others. Since the major goal of hostility is to establish or reestablish one's relative standing, it is not essential that the victim be the person who originally assaulted the self; it is only necessary that the victim be put down. The hostile aggression of middle childhood is, in fact, often targeted at displaced persons or objects who had little to do with the initial assault, but who are easy targets (Fine, 1981; Olweus, 1978; Sullivan, 1953).

Jack, a hostile aggressive child in Golding's *Lord of the Flies*, illustrates the kind of displacement to which we refer. Jack becomes hostile only after his attempts at dominance are rebuffed: first he loses out to a peer in the competition for leadership, and subsequently he fails as a hunter and is ridiculed. Jack attempts to regain power through hostile aggression toward Piggy, whom he first ridicules and belittles for his asthma ("ass-mar"), his obesity ("fatty"), his glasses, and his whining, later ostracizes and hurts (excluding from the group and taking away his glasses) and eventually murders. Piggy is a logical target because he has very low status. According to Wills, low status individuals are the ones most often targeted for downward comparison processes, because they offer the safest self-enhancing standard of comparison.

A similar conclusion is drawn by Olweus (1978), based on his extensive study of hostile aggressive children and their victims:

> For a boy with bullying tendencies, the potential whipping boy is an ideal target. His anxiousness, defenselessness, and crying give the bully a marked feeling of superiority and supremacy, also a sort of satisfaction of vague revengeful impulses. (p. 142)

Wills's theory helps explain the prevalence of competitiveness in the middle childhood period. Through competition, children can increase the difference between themselves and others, and thereby profit from downward comparison. Research indicates that children aged 8-10 are significantly more rivalrous than are 5- to 6-year-olds in the sense that they will attempt to lower the outcomes of their peers, *even if it means sacrificing their own absolute gain*. By contrast, younger children seek to maximize their own absolute gain even at the expense of relative gain (Kagan & Madsen, 1976; see also McClintock et al., 1977; Toda et al., 1978).

Awareness of social comparison processes is probably a major factor in the shift from preschoolers' competition for purposes of maximizing gain to grade-schoolers' competition as an autonomous motive (Knight et al., 1985). Grade-schoolers often seek to assert their power—their *relative* ability or *potential* to influence outcomes—rather than to cause absolute and immediate outcomes. At younger ages, fights serve mainly to settle disputes over tangible gain involving objects and territory; at older ages fights are battles for standing and status—for example, for power. It is not until the beginning of the grade school years that children can reflect upon the dominance hierarchy (Fine, 1981), and concern themselves with consistent hierarchical relationships (Omark & Edelman, 1975). Corresponding to this development is a change in the form of fighting, from the everyday instrumental skirmishes of early childhood to the more public, symbolic, and ritualized ego and status contests of middle childhood (Fine, 1981).[1] Grade-schoolers are invested in these contests when they see themselves as having efficacy in their abilities (Perry, Perry, & Rasmussen, 1986).

CAUSALITY AND INFERIORITY

The increased understanding of relative ability that begins to emerge between the ages of 5 and 7 years can, following repeated failure, lead to enduring feelings of inferiority. Grade school children can more easily use information regarding prior failure to infer a lack of ability than can younger children (Parsons & Ruble, 1977; Nicholls & Miller, 1983; Stipek & Hoffman, 1980). Grade school children are also able to use feedback regarding others' success in determining the difficulty of a task and the degree of ability that is required for success. For example, if most children do well at a task, it must be easy; failure on that task is especially likely to lead to estimations of low ability (Nicholls & Miller, 1983).

More generally, grade school children's greater reliance on relative, consensually agreed-upon standards, such as performance norms (see Nicholls & Miller, 1983 for a review) and grades (Harter, 1981) makes it more difficult to escape the reality of inferior performance and, when it continues, inferior ability. By contrast, because preschoolers rely on personal, idiosyncratic standards, "the implication of any given outcome for one's ability is obscure" (Nicholls & Miller, 1983, p. 952). Understanding the concept of ability and related concepts, such as task difficulty and effort, gives children who feel inferior real conviction in their self-estimations. "The development of the concept of ability as capacity (as compared to the absence of this concept), should mean that performance of low ability should 'feel' worse and make future failure seem more inevitable"[2] (Nicholls & Miller, 1984, p. 208).

Corresponding to the foregoing developments is an increased incidence of passive and withdrawn behaviors reflecting perceived inferior ability. Boggiano and Ruble (1979) manipulated the feedback given to grade-schoolers regarding their relative performance. Among 8- to 10-year-olds, relative failure (i.e., compared to others) led to less persistence at a task than did relative success. There were no persistence decrements for 4- to 5-year-olds, except when they failed to meet an *absolute standard* (i.e., a fixed criterion). Thus a competitive disadvantage is more likely to produce passive, withdrawn behavior in grade-schoolers than in preschoolers. Dusek, Mergler, and Kermis (1976) found that, when given a difficult memory "test," highly anxious fourth and sixth graders were more likely to attend to task irrelevant stimuli (i.e., incidental learning) than were their low-anxious peers; corresponding differences between high- and low-anxious second graders were not obtained. Dusek et al. maintain that anxious children attend to task irrelevant stimuli so as to remove themselves from the central evaluative task (p. 206). The developmental differences may reflect older children's greater awareness and avoidance of *relative* failure and their greater awareness of ability as capacity.

The research of Ruble and her colleagues suggests that grade school children are likely to avoid the embarrassment of inferiority by seeking anonymity. For example, in one study (cited in Ruble, 1983), children who had experienced relative failure, compared to children who had not, were especially likely to select an unknown future competitor instead of a competitor whom they knew.[3] This finding emerged for second and fourth graders, but not for kindergarteners. A propensity for perceiving the self as inferior may mediate this desire for anonymity. Based on findings from a subsequent observational study, Frey and Ruble (1985) conclude: "once children have developed a belief that ability is a general factor observable in all academic performance (which occurs around the second grade), a new self-consciousness regarding performance evaluation may result. Children may inhibit public evaluation in order to avoid possible embarrassment to themselves or others" (p. 560). A key variable that appears to mediate passivity, withdrawal, and task avoidance by grade school children in the aforementioned studies is their heightened concern about their *relative ability* (Parsons & Ruble, 1977; Ruble, 1983). Preschoolers also manifest passivity and withdrawal, but they do so primarily in situations in which failure to meet *absolute* standards (e.g., to complete a task) is made salient (Stipek, 1981b).

In middle childhood, the "entity view" of ability is said to emerge (Dweck & Elliott, 1983); this is the belief that one's abilities are *stable internal* attributes. Along with the entity view comes concerns about relative ability and efforts to avoid judgments of relative inability. Passive and withdrawn grade school children have been found to estimate the performance of others as superior to their own, even in the absence of actual performance differences (Dweck & Elliott, 1983).

There are also changes in reaction to failure from grade school to adolescence. Adolescents frequently attribute their failure to uncontrollable forces, such as chance, and this can help defend against low self-esteem. Preadolescents are unlikely to invoke chance attributions in explaining outcomes (Nicholls & Miller, 1985; Weisz, 1986). Even on totally noncontingent tasks, second to sixth grade children do *not* defend their self-esteem by attributing failure to bad luck (Nicholls & Miller, 1985). Similarly, grade school children blame themselves for failure on tasks that are blatantly unfair (e.g., Gray-Little, 1980). Their limited understanding of random sampling (Nicholls & Miller, 1985;

Piaget & Inhelder, 1975; Weisz, 1986), makes them more likely to evaluate negatively their capacity on the basis of unfair comparisons and unfounded social norms. This relates to Ross's (1981) findings of a marked increase from ages 5-8 and a decline throughout adolescence (15-20 years) in "unbridled use of dispositional constructs." Grade-schoolers often fail to use situational cues (e.g., involving behavior-outcome contingencies) to temper conclusions regarding dispositions (e.g., intelligence) because of their difficulty in coordinating situational and dispositional information. For example, when drawing conclusions about their ability, grade-schoolers are more likely than are adolescents to compare themselves to others who have a distinct performance advantage (Piaget & Inhelder, 1975).

Another relevant developmental difference is that problems in self-esteem center on perceived deficits in specific skills for grade-schoolers, but on perceived personality traits for adolescents (Rosenberg, 1979). This suggests that grade school children may be most prone to passivity and withdrawal when they believe they performed relatively poorly in a situation involving a specific skill, and that adolescents may be most prone to passivity and withdrawal when they believe they have performed poorly in a situation involving a complex personality trait or competency.[4] Interestingly, deficits in specific academic skills (e.g., reading) have been linked to psychiatric disorders in 10-year-olds, but not in adolescents (Rutter, Graham, Chadwick, & Yule, 1976).

Consistent with the foregoing speculation, manipulations designed to induce helplessness in grade school children frequently entail failure at concrete problems at which others are assumed to have done better than the self (Diener & Dweck, 1978) or at which they are told that others performed better (Rholes et al., 1980). By contrast, helplessness manipulations in late adolescence (college students) often entail poor performance at tasks that subjects are led to believe assess a major dimension of personality or intelligence (e.g., Carver, Blaney, & Scheier, 1979).[5] Similarly, in explaining failure, adolescents are likely to blame complex, dispositional characteristics more than specific behaviors (Peterson, Schwartz, & Seligman, 1981).

There are parallel age group differences in the standards used for assessing abilities. While grade school children rely on norms, their norms are closely tied to immediate external data—for example, how others are doing and teachers' evaluations (Dweck & Elliott, 1983). Adolescents, as compared to grade school children, have been found to rely on standards that are more complex, more internal, less closely tied to immediate cues, and more stable (Dweck & Elliott, 1983; Heckhausen, 1981; Nicholls, 1979b; Wine, 1982).

Grade-schoolers' investment in specific abilities may also make them susceptible to self-defeating behaviors in the social realm. They are more aware than are preschoolers of social abilities, such as skills at attracting attention, and more invested than are adolescents in such specific abilities. This presents particular problems for grade school unpopular children who are deficient at conventional social skills (Dodge et al., 1983). To compensate for their deficits, they may cultivate non-normative, socially inappropriate attention-getting abilities (e.g., playing the class clown). Similarly, grade-schoolers are probably more aware of and invested in their ability to influence powerful others. Grade-schoolers may actively pursue inferior status if they believe that in so doing they can increase their potential future support (e.g., by serving as a bully's sidekick/lackey or a teacher's pet).

While children of other ages also exhibit these self-defeating behaviors, their underlying motivation appears to differ. Preschoolers are more concerned than are grade-schoolers with their immediate influence and much less concerned with their ability—their *potential* influence over others and over outcomes. Adolescents, on the other hand, are less concerned with specific abilities and more concerned with general competencies and roles.

SUMMARY

Both hostile aggression and inferiority reflect grade school children's increased awareness of and concern about their potential causal influence. They are particularly concerned with a crucial abstraction: their relative status vis-à-vis specific attributes, like reading ability or social attractiveness. Hostile aggression reflects downward comparison processes in which the individual attempts to gain or regain status. In early childhood, aggression more often entails efforts to gain specific objects and privileges, and in adolescence aggression more often entails efforts to shape or resist the influence of complex institutions or systems. Inferiority results from increased awareness of relative failure and relative inability. Children who feel inferior seek anonymity and engage in passive, withdrawn, and task-inappropriate behaviors. Inferiority is especially common in middle childhood because many grade-schoolers are invested in assessing their abilities relative to others, but make unsystematic and unfairly unfavorable comparisons between themselves and others. Self-defeating behaviors are common in middle childhood because many grade-schoolers respond to perceived inferiority with socially inappropriate efforts to get attention and to influence powerful others.

NOTES

1. In middle childhood, competition is fueled by the fact that everyone is assessed in terms of the same simple skills, such as knowledge of multiplication tables and running speed (Rosenberg, 1979). By contrast, in adolescence, competition and hostile assaults are more likely to occur when children are compared in terms of larger traits—entailing values, beliefs, and general competencies. Moreover, adolescents' competitive efforts to elevate their standing often involves attempts to put down the value of others' traits as well as to put down how well others' fulfill the traits (see Rosenberg's, 1979, notion of psychological centrality). For example, street-corner youth derogate the value of the middle-class peer's sociability—their various forms of politeness and conventionality (Schwendinger & Schwendinger, 1985).

2. Because performance anxiety is closely associated with expectations of failure (Dweck & Wortman, 1982; Nicholls, 1976b; Wine, 1982) and expectations of failure are rare in preschoolers (see Dweck & Elliott, 1983 and Weisz, 1986, for reviews), it is not surprising that performance anxiety is more prevalent in middle than early childhood.

3. Although the study was concerned with strategies for maximizing success, rather than with anonymity, Ruble (personal communication) believes that embarrassment was a possible mediating factor.

4. The finding that depressive symptoms in childhood, while much less intense and longlasting than in adolescence, may actually be *more* frequent (see Lefkowitz & Burton, 1978, for a review) may also reflect grade school children's heightened vulnerability to negative appraisals of specific aspects of the self.

5. Related speculations have been offered by others. For example, (a) Dweck and Elliott (1983) observe, "In our research with grade school children we have been continually impressed with how subject . . . they are to helplessness by relatively subtle experimental manipulations. . . . We suspect however that in adolescence when children form more coherent pictures of themselves and characterize themselves in terms of even more generalized and stable characteristics, some of these tendencies may become more resistant to change" (p. 677); (b) Similarly, Ruble (1983) notes, "The study of social comparison is of greatest interest during childhood . . . once children have defined their capabilities and characters, subsequent information received . . . is likely to have less impact" (p. 136).

8

BELIEFS ABOUT INTENTIONALITY AND MIDDLE CHILDHOOD PROBLEMS

INTENTIONALITY IN MIDDLE CHILDHOOD: PRIVATE VERSUS PUBLIC DISPLAYS

In Lewis Carroll's *Alice in Wonderland*, Alice meets a mouse and, seemingly inadvertently, says a number of things that offend the mouse—such as mentioning cats—despite repeated reminders to herself to be more sensitive. Alice is dimly aware of intentions that are at odds with one another; she does not want to offend the mouse, but at the same time she has a definite dislike of mice.

When children, like Alice, become aware of competing intentions, the stage is set for a real understanding of the separation between intentions and actions (Harris & Olthof, 1982). Alice's awareness of competing intentions makes her aware that not all of her intentions can be translated into behavior. As children enter the grade school period, they increasingly view intentions as internal and private events that predispose behaviors rather than directly cause behaviors (e.g., Donaldson & Westerman, 1986; Keasey, 1977; Peevers & Secord, 1973; Rotenberg, 1980). For example, 6- to 13-year-olds, but not younger children, realize that anger predisposes a person to increased effort and decreased avoidance, and that sadness predisposes almost opposite behaviors (Aboud, 1985).

In middle childhood many youngsters come to appreciate that external expression can be dramatically at odds with internal emotional experience (Harris & Olthof, 1982; Saarni, 1984). As Selman's (1980,

p. 38) research indicates, not until middle childhood "are persons understood to have a dual layered social orientation; visible appearance possibly put on for show and a truer hidden reality." The popular magazine, *Mad*, is appreciated by children of this age partly because it pokes fun at the public/private discrepancy (e.g., Mad Magazine, 1983). Sullivan (1953, p. 220) noted "a very important discrimination which grows in the child (from early to middle childhood) between what can be expressed, demonstrated, shown, or said, in contrast to what goes on but must be treated as if it did not." For example, people often try to convince others that their private feelings are altruistic or well-meaning, while secretly harboring self-serving desires.

Recognition of the distinction between private emotion and public expression leads to awareness of "display rules"—conventions regarding which emotions should be expressed in which situations. In the grade school years, children understand the need for (a) intensifying positive affect (e.g., exaggerating positive reactions when receiving a gift), (b) minimizing pleasurable affect (e.g., not "gloating" after defeating a competitor), (c) dissimulation of affect (e.g., feigning belligerence when fearful), (Saarni, 1979, 1984; Malatesta, 1981). Consistent with the growing awareness of the public expression/private intention distinction are findings that younger children (4- to 6-year-olds) base inferences about emotion on the most obvious, public components of emotion, especially facial expression, whereas preadolescents are more likely to base inferences on more subtle cues (Gnepp, 1983; see also Harris, Olthof, & Terwost, 1981), as indicated in the next example.

The fictional character Tom Sawyer uses his new found ability to conceal his true intentions as a means of manipulating his friends into doing his work for him. He feigns great pleasure at what he regards as an odious task—painting his aunt's picket fence. He even charges his friends for the opportunity to help him. His outward affect and behavior belie his true intentions, thus enabling him to exert power over others.

Empirical findings indicate that recursive awareness of intention (i.e., "I know that you know that I know . . . ") develops during middle childhood, and that it allows for this type of manipulation of others (Flavell, 1968). As compared to preschoolers, children aged 6-13 are more likely to give misleading clues to others and to anticipate receiving such clues in a competitive situation (Shultz & Cloghesy, 1981).

As a result of their increased perspective-taking ability, grade-schoolers realize that their public displays of intention are often the object of others' scrutiny and evaluation. They thus seek to bring their public displays into line with others' expectations and social norms. For example, second and third graders' donations are influenced by the presence of an evaluative adult (i.e., a manipulation designed to increase awareness of others' perspective), but the same manipulation does not increase the donations of first graders (Froming, Allen, & Jensen, 1985). Preschoolers rely more on absolute, egocentric standards and, as noted in Chapter 11, adolescents rely more on private, internal standards.

INTENTIONALITY AND
HOSTILE AGGRESSION

Older children are more aware than are preschoolers of their own and others' intent to achieve superiority. Grade-schoolers' awareness of their own and others' ongoing, private dispositions for superiority that are in competition with one another fuels hostile aggression. Wills (1981, p. 258) reviews several studies that indicate "that the essential nature of aggression-evoking stimuli is ego threat: an *intentional*, personal insult to the subject" (emphasis added). While hostile aggression can occur in the absence of others' intentional provocation, the latter is likely to exacerbate hostile aggression. Intentional assaults are retaliated against because they pose a greater threat to the self's ongoing intentions and power than do accidental assaults.

There are a few studies indicating that the intentionality of insults is of greater concern to older than to younger children. Shantz and Vogdanoff (1973) found that 9- to 12-year-olds respond with more retaliatory aggression following intentional as compared to accidental provocation, whereas 7-year-olds react similarly to both. Ferguson and Rule (1980) found that eighth graders, but not second graders, viewed intended aggression as more reprehensible than foreseeable but unintentional aggression. Karniol (1985) found that grade school children, but not kindergarten children, derogated victims of poverty to the extent that the victims were perceived to have a choice regarding their poverty. Having choice implies that the condition of poverty was not wholly unintended. Finally, Weiner, Graham, Stern, and Lawren (1982) found that 7-year-olds were more likely than were 5-year-olds to attribute a teacher's anger at a student to the student's intentionally poor performance. There is some evidence that the tendency to focus on intentions (e.g., effort) as the cause of outcomes peaks at the end of middle childhood and declines thereafter; in adolescence relatively greater emphasis is placed on stable characteristics (Covington & Omelich, 1979; Nicholls, 1976a; Sohn, 1977)—especially in competitive situations (Parsons, 1974; Weiner & Peter, 1973).

The prevalence of hostile aggression is, in part, owing to grade schoolers' perceptions of intentional insult or injury by others in the absence of actual intent. As Dodge (1983) has shown, grade-schoolers are especially likely to aggress when they perceive that they have been intentionally aggressed against. Children who manifest the most aggression, Dodge found, are those who are especially likely to perceive hostile intent when cues regarding another's intentions are ambiguous. Given older children's recognition of the dissimulation of intentions, they have reason to distrust the expressed intentions of others (e.g., "it was an accident"), especially when other cues as to the intentionality of the assault are ambiguous.

Recognition of the private intention/public display discrepancy helps explain a common form of competition or one-upmanship engaged in by grade school children: exposing others' intentions while concealing their own. Several types of hostile aggression, such as taunting, teasing, daring, and ridiculing, can be seen as attempts to unmask others' affective displays so as to gain power. This process is illustrated in the novel *Lord of the Flies,* where Jack and Piggy are locked in a contest of wills over Jack's efforts to dominate the group. Piggy tries publicly to present himself as intending to preserve rules of fairness (e.g., fair participation in assemblies). Jack draws attention away from this intention by taunting Piggy about fatness and fears. In so doing he exacerbates and highlights Piggy's hidden intentions—to protect himself from ridicule regarding fatness and fears. Jack gains dominance over Piggy by exposing Piggy's underlying intentions.

Understandably, it becomes important in the grade school years to prevent one's own unmasking. Aggressive grade-schoolers' presentations of themselves as "tough" can be seen as an attempt to keep others at arm's distance so as to prevent exposure of their own underlying intentions—for example, to be liked or to be nurtured (Olweus, 1978; Patterson, 1982; Sullivan, 1953).

Exposing intentions may also involve exposing vulnerabilities. If others know too much about one's intentions and vulnerabilities, one's power is jeopardized. In *Lord of the Flies,* Jack tries very hard to steel himself against public demonstrations of weakness. After failing to kill a pig and humiliating himself by expressing his feelings of insecurity, he subsequently assumes the posture of the ruthless hunter and warrior.

The concealment of intentions, borne of self-presentational concerns and potential vulnerability, is foreign to the mind of the preschooler. As noted by Fine (1981, p. 37), "It is during preadolescence with its concern with peer status, that this ability and desire to position oneself in situations so as to affect one's self presentation becomes critical" (see Froming et al., 1985).

Elsewhere Fine (1981, p. 46) observes, "Insults seem to be expressed as much for reasons of self-presentation to one's peers as to attack the target." Public displays of cruelty seem often to reflect grade-schoolers' increased awareness of their peers' lust for aggression (see Olweus, 1978). Just as grade school children increase their prosocial behavior in the presence of audiences (usually adults) who expect prosocial behaviors, they are likely to increase their antisocial behavior in the presence of audiences (usually peers) who expect antisocial behaviors (see Froming et al., 1985, for a discussion of these dynamics).

INTENTIONALITY AND INFERIORITY

As they enter the grade school years, children become increasingly aware of their own and others' intentions to avoid inferiority in both social and achievement situations. Grade school children at the bottom of an ability hierarchy, unlike preschoolers of similar status, are acutely aware of their relative failure to carry out their own intentions. Since young children often infer intentions from outcomes, they are more likely to see themselves as not caring about success after experiencing failure (Nicholls & Miller, 1984). By contrast, older children's awareness that their intention to avoid inferiority is a stable disposition (Livesley & Bromley, 1973; Peevers & Secord, 1973; Rotenberg, 1980), combined with their awareness of competition in this regard between their own intentions and others' (Shultz & Cloghesy, 1981), is likely to sharpen their feelings of inferiority.

Further contributing to these feelings is grade schoolers' under-standing of the denial mechanism. Chandler, Paget, and Koch (1978) found that concrete operational children (mean age, 9 years) but not preoperational children (mean age, 6.3 years) were able to explain why an actor would deny or repress thoughts or emotions in stressful situations. This ability to "decode" or "unmask" simple psychological defenses may render the mechanisms less effective. Thus it is not surprising that denial of negative emotions is a more common strategy in preschoolers than grade-schoolers (Glasberg & Aboud, 1982; Harter & Buddin, 1987).

Grade school children may also lack some key strategies for avoiding inferiority that are often employed by adolescents. Rholes et al. (1980) and Miller (1985) found that it is not until the end of the grade school period that children experiencing repeated failure realize that decreased effort enables them to defend against assaults to their self-esteem. Prior to approximately age 12, children mistakenly assume that effort relates positively to ability. They do not fully comprehend the inverse relationship between effort and ability—that is, that the harder an individual has to try to succeed at a task, the worse are the implications for his ability at the task (see Nicholls & Miller, 1984, and Rholes et al., 1980, for reviews). In Miller's (1985) study of second and sixth graders, only the sixth graders, and among them only those who understood this inverse relationship, responded to failure by decreasing their effort (giving up) on a subsequently administered anagrams task. Their apparent purpose was to protect against attributions to limited ability. Miller (1985) found additional evidence of a self-protective mechanism operating among these older children: they decreased effort only when the anagrams were of moderate difficulty, *not* when the anagrams were extremely difficult. If they truly felt helpless, they would have been most likely to give up on the extremely difficult tasks. Failure at moderately difficult tasks, as compared to failure on extremely difficult tasks, is more likely to lead to a perception of the self as lacking in ability.

The self-protective mechanisms investigated in these studies appear to emerge about the time of entry into adolescence. Thus grade school children may be caught in an awkward transition stage: They are too old simply to deny intentions but too young to understand and employ sophisticated self-protective mechanisms—for example, to use to one's advantage the inverse relationship between effort and ability.

Because of their awareness of the distinction between private intentions and the public display of intentions, grade-schoolers are likely to try to manipulate the latter. For example, the negative expectations so frequently expressed by grade-schoolers (Dweck & Wortman, 1982; Nicholls, 1976b; Wine, 1982) may reflect attempts to present themselves as having modest goals and, ultimately, to prevent a public image of themselves as failing to meet expectations.

Grade-schoolers' awareness of the private-public distinction may also help explain the tendency of inferior children to invite victimization.

Grade school inferior children expect to be dominated, if not actively put down, by their peers. To gain a sense of power, these children may publicly present themselves as having intentions consistent with their expectations, even when this public presentation requires intentionally making the self a scapegoat, whipping boy, or butt of humor.

The following excerpt from a case analysis (Malmquist, 1983) illustrates the foregoing dynamic:

> A rather large 10-year-old girl with minimal social skills had become the butt of masochistic teasing by her classmates. While the other girls wore tennis shoes and jeans, she wore adult-looking leather shoes and dresses. . . .
>
> Her peer group had extended its attack beyond name-calling to pushing her down so that smaller children could jump on her back. . . . The girl . . . first began treatment with loud singing and banging; when these were not condemned, she asked whether she could suck her thumb "since mother always gets mad when I do it." An important phase of treatment dealt with her role as rejected buffoon, a role which she acted out in school and in the neighborhood. . . .
>
> By manipulating others to hurt her verbally or physically, the child exercised a measure of control over her environment. . . . By her clumsy belittling of herself, she was able to "make" others tease her or "put her down." Others could do no greater damage than she could do to herself. Reich described the clown as someone who makes others laugh, but is never humiliated since he induces the laughter. (pp. 202-203)

Preschoolers are less likely to participate in their victimization because they are less aware of public perspectives, and they are less invested in publicly presenting themselves as intending to behave in accord with outcomes. Self-victimization is also less likely among adolescents, who are able to understand that their "willing" victimization is in conflict with private standards regarding self-respect and personal integrity (see Chapter 11).

As noted in Chapter 6, inferiority is not always manifested in self-victimization. Socially inferior/unpopular children are also likely to manifest disagreeable, socially negative behavior. Here again it is possible that public self consciousness plays a key role. Consider the case in which children have repeatedly attempted and failed to engage in positive social behavior (e.g., to win friends). If children believe that the discrepancy between social norms (to display positive behavior) and their current functioning (displays of negative behavior) is large, they are likely to abandon efforts to narrow the discrepancy (Carver &

Scheier, 1981). Public self-consciousness heightens children's focus on this discrepancy, which further fuels the desire to give up (i.e., to abandon efforts to behave in socially positive ways; Carver & Scheier, 1981).

SUMMARY

Grade school children view intentions as predisposing actions and they are self-conscious about their public displays of intention. Hostile aggression is intended to demonstrate potential domination over others; it is particularly likely when children perceive that others intend to assault them. The cruelty and toughness of the hostile aggressive child is often in the service of exposing others' underlying intentions and concealing his or her own. In so doing, the aggressive child's relative vulnerability is minimized. Hostile aggression also leads to power when it conveys an intention to behave in ways that peers desire—for example, to satisfy peers' lust for cruelty.

By contrast, the self-defeating behavior associated with inferiority reflects awareness of the intent to avoid failure and a perceived inability to satisfy this intent. Children experiencing inferiority are unable to deny their frustrations but at the same time they lack sophisticated mechanisms for defending against attributions to inability. Their self-defeating behaviors may reflect an attempt to present a public image of themselves as intending and thus having control over negative outcomes. Grade-schoolers' consciousness of their public presentations can lead them to intentionally engage in socially unacceptable behavior when they believe that they will not succeed at socially acceptable behavior.

PART IV

THE AGE OF FREEDOM

9

PROBLEMS OF ADOLESCENCE (13-21 YEARS): REBELLION AND DEPRESSION

REBELLION

Shakespeare's character, Hamlet, in his famous soliloquy, reflects on a dilemma: He has discovered that his uncle, the new king, murdered Hamlet's father, the former king. Further complicating the dilemma are Hamlet's uncle's recent marriage to Hamlet's mother, and Hamlet's inability to share his intimate secrets with his fiancee. In response to this predicament, Hamlet considers "tak(ing) arms against a sea of troubles and, by opposing, end them." This is his rebellious option: It entails resistance against complex targets (i.e., a sea of troubles).

Rebellion is defined as organized resistance against conventions, beliefs, and institutions. In adolescence, the targets of rebellion are typically established authority or traditions, especially major societal institutions, such as family, education, religion, and political, social, economic, and legal systems. Rejection of the family is seen, for instance, in increased frequency of running away from home (Achenbach & Edelbrock, 1981). Rejection of school is seen in increased truancies. According to parents of clinic referred children, the incidence increases from about 19% at age 10-11 to about 40% at ages 14-15 (Achenbach & Edelbrock, 1981). Self-report, teacher report, and administrative statistics confirm a marked increase in truancy and absconding in adolescence (Rutter & Giller, 1984).

Involvement in civil disobedience and in religious cults may also reflect rebellion against governmental institutions and established religions, respectively. Adolescents are particularly well-represented in these forms of protest. Adolescents are substantially more likely to approve of protests, sit-ins, law refusal, and obstructing the government with mass action than are young adults (25- to 34-year-olds), or older groups (Seagull, 1977). Conventions governing sex, communication, etiquette, work, leisure, and other aspects of everyday life are also common targets of rebellion. Beech and Schoeppe (1974) found that entry into adolescence is accompanied by decreased valuing of behavior connoting conformity to convention or authority (e.g., helpfulness, obedience). Although at times adolescents oppose specific objects or events (e.g., a certain form of dress, music or family outings) these objects or events often seem to be symbolic of larger "life style" concerns.

Alcohol and drug abuse rise dramatically during adolescence—from near zero percent at ages 10-11 to between 10% (nonclinic-referred children) and 50% (clinic-referred children) at ages 14-15 (Achenbach & Edelbrock, 1981). These figures are based on parent reports; true prevalence may be somewhat different.

Drug use in adolescence is accompanied by: (a) alienation from and criticism of major goals of conventional institutions (Jessor & Jessor, 1973), (b) valuing of independence (Jessor & Jessor, 1973), nonconformity to adult expectations, and rebelliousness as measured by peer report and self-report (Brook, Whiteman, Gordon, & Cohen, 1986; Kandel, Kessler & Margulies, 1978), and (c) unconventional political and religious views (Plant, 1981). Drug-taking does not peak in incidence until the end of the adolescent period—ages 18-25 (Fishburne & Cisin, 1980).

A major form of adolescent rebellion is "socialized aggression." Hewitt and Jenkins (1946) use this term to refer to children who (a) are aggressive as a part of group activity; and (b) direct their misbehavior at societal rules of property right and conduct codes rather than against other persons. Socialized delinquency is reflected in bad companions, gang activities, cooperative stealing, furtive stealing, habitual school truancy, truancy from home and staying out late nights. In a large-scale survey, Hewitt and Jenkins (1946) found substantially more of these behaviors in adolescence (ages 13-17) than prior to adolescence (ages 6-12). By contrast, the incidence of unsocialized aggression, which resembles the hostile aggression described in the last section (i.e., assaultive tendencies, initiatory fighting, cruelty, defiance of authority, malicious mischief, inadequate guilt feelings) is more than twice as high at 6-12 years than at 13-17 years. (See Aman & Werry, 1984, and Jenkins, 1968, for similar findings.)[1]

As indicated previously, the aggression of adolescents is expressed in groups more often than is the aggression of grade-schoolers (Loeber, 1982). Tightly knit groups provide both an organization for rebellious behavior and an organized set of anticonventional beliefs (Gold & Petronio, 1980). Surveys of delinquent gangs reveal a preponderance of adolescent members' entry is typically made after puberty (Cartwright, Tomson, & Schwartz, 1975; Rutter & Giller, 1984). Parents of adolescents are considerably more likely than are parents of younger children to identify "hanging around with children who get into trouble" as a problem for their youngsters (Achenbach & Edelbrock, 1981). There is also evidence that rebellious youth are attracted to extremist groups and movements, including religious ones (Simmonds, 1977).

Rutter (1980), who uses the term *delinquency* to refer to a phenomenon similar to socialized aggression, observes: "Of all behaviors, delinquency is perhaps most striking as an adolescent phenomenon. It reaches its peak rate for males at 15 years and for females at 14 years. The rate remains high during the whole of the teenage period but then falls rapidly during early adult life" (p. 43). Consistent with Rutter's claim, indictable offenses in England increase sharply from age 10 to age 14-15, and decrease thereafter; the number of such offenses is four times greater in adolescence than in the grade school years or early adulthood (Rutter, 1980). Similarly, in the United States, youngsters aged 16-18 show higher arrest rates than does any other age group (U.S. Department of Justice, 1979).

The preceding figures have been questioned for several reasons: (a) by law young children cannot be convicted; (b) the police may be less likely to prosecute young offenders than older ones, and (c) figures for adolescents are swelled by the inclusion of status offenses (e.g., truancy, running away from home)—acts that are not illegal when committed by adults. However, data from "central registers of delinquents," which includes all children in the community referred to agencies for delinquent-type behavior, shows that the modal age of delinquent activity is 13-14 (Robison, 1960). Also, boys and girls aged 18 years admit to having committed five times more nontrivial delinquent acts in the most recent three years than do 11-year-olds (Gold & Reimer, 1975). When crimes other than status offenses are examined, adolescents still are more heavily represented than are other age groups (U.S. Department of Justice, 1979).

Stealing, which makes up the majority of indictable offenses, increases markedly from middle childhood to adolescence (Rutter, 1980; Shapland, 1978). While not always rebellious, stealing often represents an attack on societal institutions (Cloward & Ohlin, 1960; Matza, 1964; Redl & Wineman, 1957).

The following case study highlights several features of adolescent rebellion (Ralston & Thomas, 1974). "Harry," a black 18-year-old, left home after a family quarrel, and subsequently failed to communicate with his parents. His rebellious behaviors grew largely out of racial tension in his predominantly white high school.

[From his sophomore to his senior year] Harry's thinking and behavior underwent a radical change. He dropped out of the athletic program, stating that sports were the only areas where whites would accept blacks, and he wasn't going to "play Whitey's games for Whitey's school."... He joined several organizations in the city that his parents disapproved of, since they were composed primarily of radical blacks.

His parents were concerned about Harry's falling grades, his sudden change (toward less conventional) vocational plans, his new friends of questionable reputation and background, and his emphasis upon his blackness. For his part, Harry accused his parents of selling out to the white world, and having no pride in being black . . . Harry laughed at the idea that education would help improve the life of the blacks, because they still could not get jobs even if they had proper education. . . .

Currently, Harry's interests and recreation all center around the group with which he is living. They are all actively working to improve conditions for blacks living in the ghetto. Some of their projects include a day-care center for working mothers, helping blacks register to vote and campaigning for black politicians. Several weeks ago, he was arrested in a demonstration in a white-owned grocery store in the ghetto.

In summary the authors note:

Harry has rebelled against society in general and against his parents' philosophy in particular. He has decided to be militantly black and is angry about a number of things: The position of most black people in our society, the way that his parents have chosen to behave in order to get along in this society, the fact that society has probably forced them to behave this way. . . . Harry left home in order to . . . change society. (pp. 145-151)

DEPRESSION

The rebellious option is not the only one Hamlet considers; he also reflects upon the possibility of depression. As Hamlet states, the depressive option is "to suffer in mind the slings and arrows of outrageous fortune . . . to die, to sleep . . . and by a sleep to say we end the heartache and the thousand natural shocks which flesh is heir to. . . ." The hallmark of depression is a conviction in a negative view of the self and the world, a view that extends into the distant future. Depressives often have a negative cognitive set; they are predisposed to interpret ambiguous outcomes as personal failures (reviewed in Rutter & Garmezy, 1983). The Children's Depression Inventory, a widely used instrument, includes items tapping sadness, pessimism, sense of failure, dissatisfaction, guilt, self-dislike, self-harm, social withdrawal, indecisiveness, self-image change, work difficulty, fatigue, and anorexia (Kovacs & Beck, 1977).

In an epidemiological longitudinal study of the population of children on the Isle of Wight in the English Channel, Rutter, Tizard, & Whitmore (1981) found that the prevalence of depressed feelings rose from 10% at 10 years of age to about 40% at ages 14-15. Sharp increases were also found in moodiness, misery, and self-deprecation; and depressive syndromes were several times more frequent among adolescent than preadolescent children. Depressed feelings were more common in adolescents than in their parents.

Several studies of depression indicate that depression is least pronounced in the preschool years and increases with age (see Kovacs & Paulauskas, 1984, and Lefkowitz & Burton, 1978, for reviews). For example, Ushakov and Girich (1972) studied children under age 7, 7- to 10-year-olds, and 11- to 13-year-olds, and found that the depressive symptoms were most fully expressed in the oldest group. Investigations of reactions following bereavement also show increasing depressive symptomatology from early childhood to adolescence (see Rutter, 1986, for a review).

Rosenberg (1979) studied depressed feelings among 1,964 children aged 8-18. Scores in the 8-11 age group were substantially lower than in the 12-18 age group, and there was very little change over the adolescent years. In addition, instability of the self-concept—a symptom of depression (Kovacs & Beck, 1977)—peaked in adolescence. Achenbach & Edelbrock (1981) found a significant increase from ages 4 to 16 in parents' reports of the following depressive symptoms: sleeps much, underactive, suicidal talk, and unhappy, sad, or depressed. In a general population survey, Kaplan, Hong, and Weinhold (1984) found that depressive feelings are more prevalent in adolescence than in earlier childhood.

In a study of a psychiatric clinic sample, only one in nine prepubertal children showed depressive symptomatology, compared to a quarter of the postpubertal children (reviewed in Rutter & Garmezy, 1983, p. 809). In a study of 7- to 13-year-old clinic-referred girls, Garber (1984) found that 70% of the 12-13 age group were depressed versus 35% to 45% for the younger age groups (7-8 and 9-11). Significant increases from the latter groups to the older group (12-13) were found for the following symptoms: inability to have fun, appetitive problems, irritability, guilt, hypoactivity, pervasive loss of interest, hopelessness, and psychomotor retardation. Using another psychiatric sample, Ushakov and Girich (1972) found a dramatic increase in complaints of depressed affect from 9- to 12-year-olds (3 of 38 children) to 14- to 17-year-olds (17 of 20 children). The incidence of diagnosed depression in hospitals steadily increases from the youngest age groups studied (10- to 14-year-olds) through midadulthood (25-44) and declines thereafter (reviewed in Weiner, 1980). However, as noted by Weiner (1980, p. 454), these figures may reflect differential willingness to refer depressed persons of different ages to these facilities or differential willingness to assign the diagnosis: "There appears to be considerable difference between the frequency with which depression is actually diagnosed in adolescents and the role it plays in their adjustment problems." Whereas fewer than 10% of adolescent patients are diagnosed as being primarily depressed, about half of them display such depressive symptoms as dysphoric affect, self-deprecation, crying spells, and suicidal thoughts or attempts (Masterson, 1967). Moreover, 35% to 40% of nonpatient samples of young people report having some feelings of sadness, worthlessness, or pessimism about the future (Albert & Beck, 1975; Murray, 1973).

Suicide attempts, which are often linked to depression (Weiner, 1980), also increase in adolescence. Attempted suicides are infrequent before puberty and peak at ages 15-19 (Hawton & Goldacre, 1982; Kreitman, 1977). At inpatient hospital psychiatric units, recent suicide attempts have been found in 10-15% of adult patients but in as many as 40% of adolescent patients (cited in Weiner, 1980). Approximately 1 in 1,000 adolescents in the general population attempts suicide each year (Seiden, 1969); the figure for grade school children and for adults is several times less. Moreover, these reports are likely to be substantially less than actual numbers.

A case illustrating key aspects of many adolescent suicide attempts is cited by Weiner (1982, p. 443).

> Sara, age 16, had been in constant conflict with her mother. . . . On New Year's Eve, as Sara was dressing for a date that had been arranged weeks in advance, her mother suddenly decided that she was not old enough and could not go. . . . Sara stayed home, crushed by this arbitrary decree, only to have her mother and stepfather subsequently go out and leave her alone. . . . [Feeling] abandoned and hopeless . . . she swallowed some barbiturates. She was careful, however, to limit herself to a small dose that only made her groggy. She went to bed and the next morning told her parents what she had done.
>
> Her mother became furious (and) called (Sara's aunt) to come over. The aunt's approach was to call Sara an actor and a fake. . . . Sara went upstairs and slashed deeply into both of her wrists with a razor blade. She then came downstairs, dripping blood to ask, "Am I faking now?"

Sara's concern over the arbitrariness of her parents' restriction and her investment in the genuineness of her own expression of intention are key control themes elaborated upon in Chapters 10 and 11, respectively.[2]

SUMMARY

Adolescents are especially susceptible to rebellion and depression. Rebellion is defined as organized resistance against conventions, beliefs, and institutions. It is evident in truancy, absconding, involvement in social protest, alcohol and drug abuse, and group delinquency. Incidence of all of these behaviors increases from middle childhood to adolescence. Depression, defined as a conviction in a negative world that extends into the distant future, is manifest in such symptoms as sadness, pessimism, and a sense of failure. Studies of nonclinic-referred children, and some studies of clinic-referred children, indicate a marked increase in depressive reactions and diagnoses of depression from pre- to middle adolescence. Suicide attempts, another symptom of depression, also increase substantially over this age span.

NOTES

1. In a follow-up study, employing more than 1,000 clinic-referred children, Jenkins (1968) found that unsocialized aggression was twice as common in children less than age 10 than in children age 10 and above, whereas socialized aggression was more common in the older group. As with the Hewitt and Jenkins study, unsocialized aggressive behaviors (e.g., disobedience with hostile component, bullying, domineering, destructiveness) resemble the hostile aggressive behaviors described in Chapter 6, whereas socialized aggressive behaviors (e.g., truancy from school, running away from home, group stealing) are more organized and directed against major societal institutions. Unfortunately, Jenkins's report of age differences in this study did not provide more precise details.

2. British, French, and American statistics indicate that the rate of successful suicides increases 100-fold from prior to age 10 to ages 10-14, and that there is a further 10-fold increase from 10-14 to 15-19 years. However, unlike suicide attempts, successful suicides continue to rise in incidence, reaching a peak in old age (reviewed in Rutter & Garmezy, 1983).

10

BELIEFS ABOUT CAUSALITY AND ADOLESCENT PROBLEMS

CAUSALITY IN ADOLESCENCE:
A SYSTEM OF INFLUENCES

Adolescents are more aware of complex causal systems than are grade-schoolers. This is reflected partly in a shift in reading preferences from novels that have unidimensional and ballistic plots to those that have multidimensional and circuitous plots. Outcomes in adolescent novels are explained by a network of conceptually linked physical and psychological causal forces. Solution of mystery novels, such as *Presumed Innocent* by Turow, requires an understanding of interactions among motives, methods, and circumstances woven together in complex plots. In the novel, several people might have been motivated to murder a particular person; one actually committed the murder but arranged clues that made others look guilty. Moreover, the complexities are layered; one who was not guilty got wind of the guilty party's actions yet did not reveal them.

Grade school children's mysteries, such as the Hardy Boys and Nancy Drew, do not involve such complex interplays of causal forces. While they occasionally entail "twists" in plot, the twists are kept to a minimum, are carefully spelled out and are not generally layered. For example, in *A Clue in the Diary*, all causal clues initially point to one suspect who, subsequently, is proven to be innocent; this single turn in plot takes the entire novel to unfold.

Armed with more sophisticated causal concepts, adolescents gain a new understanding of social forces. Compared to grade-schoolers, they have more sophisticated conceptions of cause-effect relations in such social institutions as banks, schools, and government (Furth, 1980). For example, grade school children maintain that money to run a school comes from the principal's safe. By contrast, the adolescent recognizes a system of interacting influences: teachers get money from the local government, which in turn secures money from taxes. Similarly, adolescents have a richer appreciation than do children of the organization of the school—the influences of parents, teachers, and administration on one another—and the links between the school and the larger social system of policymakers, taxpayers, and a value system.

Preadolescents generally do not understand the basic causal principles involved in the economic system (Furth, 1980). For example, they fail to note the importance of profit in maintaining a business. Grade school children have little appreciation of the need for complex economic and political solutions to poverty (Merelman, 1971). We would speculate that, because they grasp the larger economic system, adolescents are more likely to become disenchanted with simple Robin Hood formulations for resolving inequities; they are able to question the wisdom of taking away money from wealthy persons, who might otherwise invest their funds and thereby stimulate economic growth, higher employment, and other socially beneficial outcomes.

Regarding children's understanding of the political system and governmental functions, Furth concluded that, prior to adolescence, "their thinking about the general needs of a societal community . . . is concrete and therefore unsystematic" (p. 50). Adolescents are more likely than are grade-schoolers to consider systematically the short-term versus long-term benefits of policies and the cost-effectiveness of one decision relative to another (Adelson & O'Neil, 1966). Adolescents are also more aware of the complicated procedures involved in the implementation, maintenance, and alteration of the political system. Grade school children can comprehend these procedures, but not as systematically and not on as large a scale. For example, they understand the concept of compromise but they have difficulty understanding the nature and functioning of political parties and vested interests (Lewis, 1981). Similarly, grade-schoolers have a well-developed understanding of agreements (Damon, 1977), but adolescents show a fuller recognition of processes for reaching consensus, of social contracts, and of "free agreements" (Kohlberg, 1978; also see Selman, 1980). Prior to adolescence, children view government and the law principally as coercive agencies to police people. In adolescence they understand how government can be a cooperative, agreed-upon venture, and they understand factors that make this difficult. They also realize that if procedures are nonarbitrary—if the reasons for them are agreed upon—the individual will experience a sense of freedom (see Gallatin, 1980, for a review).

Most realms of the adolescent's personal and social world come to be viewed as systems. Besides the economic and political systems are the religious system (Elkind, 1971; Nye & Carlson, 1984), the system of peers and friends (Damon, 1977; Selman, 1980; Youniss, 1980), the family system (Selman, 1980; Watson & Amgott-Kwan, 1984), the system of social convention (Turiel, 1978), and the "self-system" (Harter, 1983; Selman, 1980). The latter refers to the network of self-perceived traits and competencies, as opposed to the amalgam of physical characteristics and simple skills that are of such importance to grade-schoolers. In each of these realms, adolescents are aware of complex, interacting causal influences.

As children enter adolescence, they gain a fuller understanding of the distinction between contingent and noncontingent (chance) phenomena (Nicholls & Miller, 1985; Weisz, 1986a). Adolescents become invested in contemplating the probabilities of various events (Piaget & Inhelder, 1975; Weisz, 1986a). "If I work hard, will I succeed in school/at my job?" is a more absorbing question to someone who has the intellectual wherewithal to consider the relevant probabilities than it is to one who does not. Adolescents realize that even when they decide whether to exert effort, the outcome—whether or not their effort will pay off—is at least partly determined by chance and partly by an array of other causal factors that are unrelated to their own behavior. They understand that low-probability events may occur and that high-probability events may not. Moreover, they can systematically combine probabilities—for example, the net impact of working hard when one has only modest ability, and under aversive conditions with luck tilted slightly against a favorable outcome. Adolescent understanding of contingency and probability is dependent upon the recognition of the independence of some causes and interdependence of others (Weisz, 1986a).

It is possible that adolescents' awareness of systems and contingencies is largely responsible for their concerns about freedom. When causal forces are seen as capriciously determining an individual's behavior, the individual may be especially vulnerable to a loss of perceived freedom. If adolescents perceive themselves to be "integral parts of the system," they tend to believe that they have "choice" and "freedom"; but often this is not the case (Matza, 1964, p. 11). Rebellion and depression are two extreme strategies for dealing with threats to and losses of perceived freedom.

CAUSALITY AND REBELLION

In rebellion the adolescent seeks freedom from the shackles of "the system" or "the establishment." Adolescents' resolve often surprises people invested in the system, especially those in authority, who may perceive rebellion as being directed against a particular custom rather than against an entire institution. For example, unmarried couples who live together "in sin" are likely to be seen by their more conservative parents as challenging specific sexual morals rather than the larger social institution of marriage.

To take a stand against the system, the adolescent must ultimately take a stand against all its interdependent parts. For example, Hamlet felt that in order to rebel against his uncle, he must oppose all people associated with his uncle, including his uncle's minister's daughter, who was Hamlet's fiancee. Even seemingly trivial restrictions are opposed because they represent threats to the larger principle involved. Often underlying seemingly trivial concrete issues (e.g., gum-chewing in class) are principles of individual freedom (e.g., students' rights)—principles in which adolescents are far more invested than are preadolescents (Gallatin, 1980; Turiel, 1974).

An adolescent known to the second author insisted on leaving intact an obscenity her friend had written prominently on her cast (she had an injured hand). Despite her parents' insistence that she black out or disguise the profanity, she persisted in wearing the unaltered cast to several public events, and she propped it on the dinner table when a minister and his wife visited. Her rationale for this form of rebellion had to do with freedom—her friend's freedom to express himself, her freedom to do as she pleased with her own hand, and—most importantly—her freedom to be true to herself. Clearly, the issues at stake were broader and deeper than a simple rule about obscenity.

Rebellion of this sort is frequently directed against established procedures for developing or maintaining principles. Just as the American colonists were mistakenly seen as resisting higher taxes when they were actually resisting "taxation without representation," adolescents may be seen as obstinately opposing a curfew or indulging in profanity when the larger issue is whether the curfew or rules about proper speech were decided democratically (Gallatin, 1980). The adolescent's reluctance to accept conventional procedures, such as adjudication by authority figures or group agreement, adds to the seeming irrationality of the rebellion. Adolescents are prone to reject these procedures if they have concerns about the underlying decision-making process—for example, the source of the authority figure's authority or the procedures followed by the group in reaching its agreement (Schwendinger & Schwendinger, 1985). Unless rationales are provided, decisions appear arbitrary. Adolescents who perceive their parents as failing to provide "reasons" for restrictions on individual freedoms are more likely to engage in delinquent activity than are adolescents who perceive their parents as providing reasons (Nye, 1975).

Rebellion can also be triggered by anger at noncontingent causal influences—chance, fate or an unresponsive environment. Redl and Wineman (1957), in their classic study of delinquent boys, note the frequency with which antisocial behavior was blamed on bad luck and bad fortune. Delinquents cited their feeling that they "never get a break" to justify their assault on their environment. The arbitrary and capricious quality of adolescents' misfortunes often fuels their sense of indignation and injustice and ultimately energizes their rebellion (see Matza, 1964). Of course, attributions to chance and bad breaks can often be used as after-the-fact justifications for adolescent delinquent behavior. But their use in this way, too, highlights the perceived relevance of chance within the causal framework of the adolescent.

CAUSALITY AND DEPRESSION

A common cause of depression among adolescents is the feeling of being overwhelmed by the system. Even if they act, adolescents are more aware of the forces that make it difficult for them ultimately to be masters of their own destiny. While grade-schoolers may conclude that failure is likely after experiencing a string of failures, adolescents can envision a system of forces, involving lack of ability, low effort, task difficulty, and powerful others that strengthen their expectation of future failure. This may help explain the finding that, when subjects are exposed to failure and then to tasks different than those at which they failed, children entering adolescence manifest more helplessness than do grade-schoolers (Miller, 1985; Rholes et al., 1980).

Grade-schoolers' failure to systematically entertain different casual dimensions—as evident in their difficulty attending to more than one attributional dimension at a time (Seligman & Peterson, 1986)—may serve as a buffer against serious depressive reactions. Depression in adults is most likely when negative outcomes are attributed to causes that are internal, stable *and* global (e.g., pervasive lack of ability; Abramson et al., 1978).

Feelings of helplessness can pervade one's relationships with the educational, political, and economic systems. Adolescents' awareness of a disturbed "family system" (Minuchin, 1974) and of their own enmeshment within it (Lidz, 1964) can lead to the same sense of futility that accompanies recognition of other complex and aversive social institutions. Often it is awareness of seemingly unchangeable processes responsible for maintaining the existing system, such as disturbed communications (see Bateson, Jackson, Haley, & Weakland, 1956), that lies at the heart of depression. The hopelessness and despair of downtrodden minorities often centers on their awareness of their own inability to influence the procedures underlying social, economic, and legal institutions (Brinton, 1952).

A sense that chance is working against the self can also contribute to depression. Adolescents are susceptible to what Seligman and his colleagues term "universal helplessness"—the recognition that outcomes are completely and inherently noncontingent (Abramson, Seligman, & Teasdale, 1978). Prior to adolescence, children are willing to exert effort, even on tasks involving completely noncontingent (chance-determined) outcomes, in the mistaken belief that such outcomes are influenced by ability, practice, and effort (Nicholls & Miller, 1985; Weisz, 1986a). Adolescents experience despair over adverse fate and fortune because, unlike grade-schoolers, they are aware of their inability to control the random factors involved. For example, an adolescent may ruminate about the role of chance in causing a loved one to be killed in a car accident from which the other passengers walked away unharmed. Grade school children are less able to fathom the randomness of the contingencies involved. Hamlet's soliloquy captures the plight of many adolescents: They perceive themselves as suffering from the cruel hand of fate—from "outrageous fortune"—and recognize their inability to control it. Recognition of noncontingency is thought to play a critical role in the development of depression (Abramson et al., 1978).

Adolescents are also prone to depression when they experience arbitrary aversive forces and are unable to find personal meaning in these forces (Harlow, Newcomb, & Bentler, 1986). Research on religious development (Elkind, 1971) indicates that adolescents, much more than younger children, are concerned about and seek religious meaning (e.g., "Why do bad things happen to good people?") that they are often unable to attain. Although most adolescents do not regularly reflect on such issues (Adelson, 1980; Weiner, 1980), tragedies such as the death of a loved one are likely to lead to increased effort to find causal explanations and, if this effort proves futile, to depression (Rothbaum et al., 1982; Silver & Wortman, 1980). Interestingly, there is evidence that religiosity is associated with low suicide rates (Martin, 1984).

The sense of futility that can accompany adolescents' quest for meaning is well illustrated in Achenbach's (1982) case study of Peter. Notes from Peter's journal, which was found after he committed suicide, contained the following excerpts:

> I don't know what I am, where I am, . . . what I'm doing here, and in other words, I don't know anything. I'm just one crazy mixed up kid who hasn't got the foggiest idea of what is going on. I don't understand life, love, anything. I just keep asking questions and getting nothing for answers. And it's driving me crazy. I will not be satisfied until I know all the answers. I don't even know who I am. Something must have created me. But who and why? God is supposed to be so kind and right. But what kind of creator would allow such things he has created to kill each other and be so cruel to each other? The situation on earth has gotten out of control and I want to get off. (p. 407)

SUMMARY

Adolescents recognize the existence of complex causal systems. This can be seen in their understanding of economic, political, religious, and other institutions, and in their conceptions of chance and fate. Rebellion results, in part, from an appreciation of causal complexities and a perceived need to take a stand against the system as a whole. Adolescent rebellion is often characterized by attacks directed at the source of the problem: the procedures giving rise to the system. Ultimately, rebellion is targeted against institutions and noncontingent forces that are seen as arbitrarily violating personal freedom. Depression, by contrast, reflects hopelessness about the self's ability to influence institutions and other external contingencies, because of the complex, systematic, and often random nature of the forces involved. Inability to find meaning in these complexities further contributes to despair and depression.

11

BELIEFS ABOUT INTENTIONALITY AND ADOLESCENT PROBLEMS

INTENTIONALITY IN ADOLESCENCE: CONFLICTING MOTIVES

As noted in Chapter 8, children entering the grade school era become aware that intentions do not automatically lead to outcomes and that there is a difference between private and public intentions. The next great milestone in understanding intentions, typically accompanying entry into adolescence, is that intentions exist at different levels and that they are often in conflict with one another. This awareness of contradictions in intentions is nicely articulated by the heroine of Plath's (1966) novel *The Bell Jar*; "If neurotic is wanting two mutually exclusive things at one and the same time, then I'm neurotic as hell. I'll be flying back and forth between one mutually exclusive thing and another for the rest of my life" (p. 98). The awareness of conflicting intentions is a key feature of adolescent identity formation.

Cognitive developmental research has repeatedly demonstrated the formation of an abstract psychological self—a sense of identity—in adolescence (Feather, 1980). Grade-schoolers are likely to refer to situational, behavioral, and emotional aspects of self (e.g., "I play at the playground"; "I hit my brother"; "I get mad at my mother"), whereas 15- to 20-year-olds are likely to refer to their traits, beliefs, and values (e.g., "I am really friendly"; "I think it's wrong to cheat"; Bernstein, 1980, p. 317) and to stable, psychological dispositions (Wood, 1978). Adolescents' abstract conceptions of themselves results from their rapidly increasing private self-awareness[1] (Broughton, 1978; Dollinger, Thelen, & Walsh, 1980; Inhelder & Piaget, 1958; Selman, 1980). They can consciously reflect upon their subjective experiences, and they attempt to integrate these experiences into a complex self-system (Broughton, 1978; Selman, 1980) involving underlying traits and dispositions, as well as ambivalent and conflicting motivational states (Selman, 1980).

Based on his research, Selman (1980, p. 38) concludes that children as late as "about ages 7 to 12 . . . see feeling states . . . as groupings of mutually isolated and sequential (or weighted) aspects. For example, when moving to a new neighborhood, a child might recognize herself to be 'mostly curious and happy and a little scared.'" Although grade-schoolers realize that they have different intentions, they generally regard the different intentions as separated from one another, affectively and/or temporally. They rarely recognize the relationships among and the conflicts between their various intentions.

By contrast, the adolescent seeks to resolve conflicts: between the self that is natural and the self that strives for ideals; between the real and the phony; and between the rational and the irrational (Broughton, 1978). Two significant advances are involved here: recognition of complex intentions that collectively define the "self," and attempts to resolve contradictions between components of this self-definition. Much of the teenager's self-reflection is aimed at resolving these contradictions. Based on extensive interviews, Selman (1979) concludes that adolescents perceive themselves as having a "little man" inside their minds that "can organize the self's inner psychological life" (p. 60; see Bernstein, 1980). Erikson (1968) and Marcia (1966) also provide evidence of adolescents' quest for a unified, integrated "identity" (see Broughton, 1978; Harter, 1983). Adolescents with the most diffuse sense of identity are the ones who are most self-conscious; those with a unified identity are the least self-conscious (Adams, Abraham, & Markstrom, 1987).

Several of the aforementioned researchers have found a link between adolescents' identity formation and their concerns about control. These concerns center on the "freedom" to be and to act as one "really" intends. In an example given earlier, an adolescent girl refused to draw a design on her cast to disguise an obscenity a friend had written there. One reason for her refusal was that "drawing some flowery design— that's not the real me." Adolescents' introspection allows for a monitoring and manipulation of thought processes that would be virtually "unthinkable" in middle childhood. One adolescent copes with the loss of a puppy, as follows: "I can fool myself into not wanting to have another puppy if I keep on saying to myself, 'I don't want a puppy; I don't even want to see another puppy'" (Selman, 1980, p. 103). Broughton (1978) claims that, in adolescence, the mind takes on volitional characteristics; for example, one adolescent reports "with our minds we can make judgments and do what we think is right" (Broughton, 1978, p. 87). Other researchers note a linkage between adolescent identity formation on one hand, and their ability to modify self-experience (Damon & Hart, 1982), and their awareness of self-control (Harter, 1983; Rosenberg, 1979), and self-determination (Montemayor & Eisen, 1977) on the other hand. These authors see identity formation as leading to enhanced perceptions of control.

By contrast, other investigators emphasize that adolescents' recognition of their competing intentions and standards makes the limits of conscious control very salient. Adolescents are aware that "no purposeful act of conscious effort or will can yield a total understanding of all the actions of the self" (Gardner, 1982, p. 485). The common adolescent insight that the self is very limited in its ability to change its underlying personality or character (Selman, 1979, 1980) also bespeaks a new, more sophisticated recognition of the limits of control. Often there is a conflict between the person one intends to be and the person one feels oneself really is. Siding with either of these selves poses limitations on one's sense of freedom. The vacillation resulting from efforts to resolve these conflicts (and to achieve freedom) perhaps accounts for the peaking of "instability of the self-image" during ages 12-16 (Rosenberg, 1979).

The adolescent's need for freedom to be oneself, emphasized by Broughton (1978), was illustrated by Holden Caulfield in Salinger's (1951) *Catcher in the Rye*. Holden was preoccupied with "phoniness." He had contempt for nearly everyone because he thought they pretended to possess noble, altruistic intentions when their underlying motives were base and egotistical. For example, his superintendent appeared to be concerned about the well-being of his students, but Holden believed he was really trying to get parents to donate more money to the school. Similarly, a formerly admired teacher and father figure made homosexual advances toward Holden. But Holden was most concerned with his own phoniness. He recognized his attempts to impress others with his competence, his maturity, and his altruism even though he was not self-confident in any of these respects.

Adolescents' heightened introspection raises issues of identity— "Who am I," "What do I stand for?" (Erikson, 1968; Feather, 1980)— and issues of freedom, but it does not resolve them. In fact, self-consciousness per se leaves the adolescent painfully aware of his difficulty achieving identity and freedom. Research on self-awareness supports this claim: Manipulations, such as mirrors, which are designed to increase private self-consciousness, often lead to: (a) a sense of obligation to adhere to personal standards (for a review see Carver & Scheier, 1981), (b) a decreased sense of "choice," "freedom," "self-direction," and (c) an increased sense of "situational constraints" (Diener & Srull, 1979). The disposition to private self-consciousness peaks in adolescence (Broughton, 1978; Damon & Hart, 1982; Rosenberg, 1979; Selman, 1980; Selman & Jaquette, 1978). The effects of dispositional self-consciousness are similar to the effects of experimental manipulations of self-consciousness (Brockner, 1979).

It is important to distinguish between private self-consciousness—awareness of self's private desires, beliefs, and standards—and public self-consciousness—the adoption of others' perspective on the self (see Carver & Scheier, 1981). Public self-consciousness, which increases in middle childhood (see Chapter 8), is more concerned with public, visible aspects of the self (e.g., task performance). Evidence just cited indicates that it is private rather than public self-consciousness that increases dramatically in adolescence.[2] There are paralleled findings regarding the development of personal standards (principles) and social standards (norms): the latter are frequently relied upon in middle childhood, and the former are typically not relied upon until adolescence (Dweck & Elliott, 1983; Nicholls, 1979).

There is evidence that adolescents are more affected by manipulations intended to increase private self-consciousness than are younger children. In a naturalistic study, Beaman, Klentz, Diener, and Svanum (1979) instructed Halloween trick-or-treaters to take one candy from a candy bowl. Private self-awareness was manipulated by having a mirror in front of the candy bowl for some of the trick-or-treaters. The mirror decreased the "transgression rate" (i.e., taking more than one candy) by 55% among adolescents (children 13 and above) but only by 15% for preadolescents, and not at all for younger children. Similarly, Froming et al. (1985) found that a mirror did not increase prosocial behavior—that is, number of candies donated—of grade-schoolers; but this manipulation has repeatedly been found to increase altruism in undergraduates (Carver & Scheier, 1981). Like us, Froming et al. claim that the capacity to become aware of one's own personal standards, and the resulting feeling of pressure or obligation (i.e., lack of freedom) to violate these standards, increases dramatically as the individual enters adolescence.

INTENTIONALITY AND REBELLION

Adolescent rebellion may often be associated with deindividuation—the process whereby people become less aware of their individual selves. Deindividuation increases perceived freedom by "lessening perceived restraints" (Festinger, Pepitone, & Newcomb, 1952).[3] Awareness of one's individual self (i.e., private self-consciousness) often decreases perceived freedom, especially when it reminds the individual of irreconcilable inconsistencies between intentions and standards. Since adolescents frequently feel unable to integrate the various aspects of self, they strive, accordingly, for deindividuation and other means of avoiding self-consciousness (see Steenbarger & Aderman, 1979).

Deindividuation leads to decreased self-awareness and decreased self-regulation, and to various unrestrained and impulsive behaviors that are often associated with rebellion. These include cheating and aggression (Diener & Wallbom, 1976), increased sense of spontaneity (Diener, 1979), and perceived "freedom from restraints" (Festinger et al., 1952). The main factor presumed to mediate these effects is a reduced inward focus, that is, reduced private self-consciousness (Diener, 1979). Moreover, deindividuation has been shown to be a desirable state, accompanied by feelings of activity and energy, jubilance, glee, and a willingness to participate again in the deindividuating activity (Prentice-Dunn & Rogers, 1982).

Many of the *antecedents* of deindividuation are activities and circumstances typically associated with rebellion. These include participating in and becoming part of a group, anonymity, sensory overload (e.g., from loud music or frenetic activity), and giving up or diffusing responsibility (for reviews, see Diener, 1980; Dipboye, 1977). Involvement in social movements (e.g., Hitler Youth, military organizations, extremist political and religious groups, and cults) as well as in riots, mobs, and gangs, may also be attempts to deindividuate so as to diminish private self-consciousness and increase freedom from self's inhibitions and standards. Alcohol abuse, drug abuse, and various forms of thrill-seeking also have been found to diminish private self-consciousness (Carver & Scheier, 1981; Hull & Young, 1983).

Yet another way that rebellious adolescents may reduce self-consciousness is by cultivating a seemingly impenetrable exterior. In so doing they prevent intimacy and others' scrutiny of the inner self. Clinical descriptions of delinquents (Matza, 1964; Schwendinger & Schwendinger, 1985), autobiographies focused on adolescence (e.g., Malcolm X; Claude Brown), and novels involving adolescent protagonists (e.g., *Catcher in the Rye*, *The Bell Jar*) indicate that adolescents spend considerable energy avoiding intimacy and others' scrutiny. Individuals' unwillingness to reveal themselves to others, which peaks in early adolescence (Elkind & Bowen, 1979), relates to experimental and questionnaire measures of self-consciousness (Adams et al., 1987).

A major goal of deindividuation is evidently to reduce awareness of parts of the self that are in conflict with more central aspects. Holden Caulfield's rebellion exemplifies this quest for consistency. He attempts to lose sight of his conventional intentions—which he sees as restricting his freedom to be himself and to achieve genuineness. This attempt sometimes leads to an open and honest display of impulses (e.g., leaving school, visiting a prostitute, saying whatever comes to mind). Like Salinger, the writer Jack Kerouac enjoyed great success with adolescent audiences partly by creating heroes who unabashedly pursued their underlying desires. Their incessant activity and sensation-seeking leads to a state of deindividuation in which they are less aware of internal, conventional standards. These heroes are spontaneous, uninhibited, and genuine—they do not pretend to be more virtuous than they really are—and thus avoid the pain of conflicting intentions (see Erikson, 1968; Feather, 1980).

Prosocial behavior in its extreme can also be rebellious, if it involves rejection of conflicting values held by the larger society. For example, radical Christianity is rebellious in its advocacy of total nonaggression (Haimowitz, 1966). Interestingly, deindividualized adolescents engage in more prosocial actions (administering fewer shocks to a confederate) when in the presence of cues supporting nonaggression (wearing robes resembling nurses' uniforms), than when in the absence of such cues. By contrast, deindividuated adolescents increase the number of shocks administered when the cues support aggression (wearing robes resembling Ku Klux Klan uniforms; Johnson & Downing, 1979). The key to deindividuated rebellion is not the domination of antisocial intentions, but the effort to escape feelings of restraint and to pursue uninhibitedly desires dictated by salient cues in the immediate situation (Johnson & Downing, 1979; Zimbardo, 1969).

In delinquent rebellion, the search for self-consistency is often said to take the form of a "negative identity." This occurs when antisocial beliefs and values are dominant, and form the basis for organizing the "self-system" (Selman, 1980). "Sounding," delinquents' use of challenges and insults to "probe how deep the facade of personal appearance goes" (Matza, 1964, p. 43), is a vehicle for assessing consistency between public and private intentions. Delinquents are sounded "almost incessantly" along several dimensions, such as manliness (e.g., "Are you really a man or just a kid?") and loyalty (e.g., "Are you really one of us, or just faking it?"; Matza, 1964, p. 53). Protests such as, "Man, I ain't *that* bad," when delinquents seek to excuse themselves from delinquent activity, reflect the conflict between conventional, societally sanctioned values and societally condemned gang values (Matza, 1964; Schwendinger & Schwendinger, 1985).

Rebellion can result from private self-awareness as well as from attempts to escape it. Private self-awareness often intensifies efforts to adhere to personal principles (Carver & Scheier, 1981; Inhelder & Piaget, 1958). This may contribute to the rebellious idealism described by Keniston (1967) and Erikson (1968). For example, during the 1960s, principled rebellion took the form of protests against inequities at both the national level (civil rights) and internationally (Vietnam War).

These conjectures suggest the existence of two types of rebellion—one basically egotistical (adhering to immediate desires) and one basically idealistic (adhering to personal, unconventional standards). Evidence of both types comes from studies examining individual differences in the motives and behavior of participants in rebellious activities, such as the Berkeley Free Speech Movement (Haan, Smith, & Block, 1968).

INTENTIONALITY AND DEPRESSION

Research has also linked heightened self-awareness to depression. Self-awareness can lead to increased pressure to adhere to standards, which in turn often results in increased negative affect, self-blame, perceived responsibility (Wicklund, 1975), withdrawal (Carver & Scheier, 1981), sensitivity and negative reactions to rejection (Fenigstein, 1979), feelings of helplessness (Carver et al., 1979), decreased self-esteem, and decreased perceived freedom (Diener & Srull, 1979)—all symptoms of depression. As noted earlier, self-awareness increases these depressive symptoms in situations in which individuals feel unable to achieve their private standards (Carver & Scheier, 1981).

The following case of a 17-year-old's suicide attempt illustrates how increased private self-awareness can focus attention on a negative self-image. Interestingly, the self-awareness was prompted by a mirror—the most commonly employed manipulation in laboratory studies.

> There I was, staring at that frantic face in the mirror and wondering whose it was. I realized that I was that pathetic girl with tears running down her fat, red cheeks and I hated her. I began swallowing the pills as fast as I could. All I could think of was the desire to get out of my disgusting life. (Ralston & Thomas, 1974, p. 121)

There is evidence that adolescent college students exposed to both failure and self-awareness manipulations feel and behave helplessly, whereas adolescent college students exposed to the same failure experiences in the absence of self-awareness do not feel or behave helplessly (Carver et al., 1979). The researchers argue that self-awareness leads to more aversive reactions because it focuses the individuals' attention on their standards and their failure to live up to them. Since self-awareness has little effect on grade-schoolers (Froming et al., 1985) it is a dynamic seemingly well suited to account for the relatively greater incidence of depression in adolescence (Carver & Scheier, 1981). Like the fictional self-conscious adolescents mentioned earlier—Holden and Hamlet—the adolescent subjects in self-awareness studies apparently feel helpless to resolve the discrepancy between standards and what they believe they can accomplish. One way they can cope with the discrepancy is by withdrawing from the situation.

The foregoing evidence suggests that self-conscious adolescents who are low in self-esteem are probably the ones most likely to perceive irreconcilable discrepancies between their standards and their behavior, and thus to manifest depression (see Carver & Scheier, 1981). These individuals may seek to escape their standards but escape does not ensure freedom:

> Standards or goals . . . are sometimes important even central to one's life. It is possible to disengage from them in one's thoughts . . . But the freedom to do so is not absolute . . . Without a drastic reorganization of one's value system . . . it is impossible to avoid for very long a reconfronting of psychological dimensions that are important (Carver & Scheier, 1986).

In *Catcher in the Rye*, the 15-year-old protagonist repeatedly experiences bouts of depression centered on his failure to live up to personal standards. He feels unable to live up to his standards of conduct involving interpersonal relationships (especially genuineness in heterosexual relationships) and family relationships (open communication with his parents and sister). At times, he seeks freedom by ignoring his standards and by glorifying his impulses; but ultimately this avoidance of standards is unsuccessful. Because of their self-awareness, adolescents rarely escape their standards for prolonged periods (Carver & Scheier, 1986).

At times, adolescents view their impulses (especially their sexual ones) as base, fleeting, and insubstantial, and they seek to curb if not deny them. But they cannot will away their impulses any more than they can will away their standards, and they are acutely aware of this further limitation on their freedom. Adolescents sometimes seek freedom through programs of ascetic self-denial. Adolescents who fail in attempts at self-denial are vulnerable to loss of freedom and to depression, because they realize they cannot liberate themselves from their impulses by an act of will. Suicide, which brings with it a liberation from frustrated intentions, may in part represent an extreme form of the quest to will away all desires (i.e., anhedonia). As Hamlet ponders suicide he eloquently articulates this quest: "To die, to sleep, . . . and by a sleep to say we end the heartache and the thousand natural shocks which flesh is heir to. 'Tis a consummation devoutly to be wished."

A seemingly paradoxical feature of depression is that it consists of both feelings of uncontrollability—inability to influence the environment—and self-blame (Abramson & Sackeim, 1977). Janoff-Bulman (1979) and Peterson et al. (1981) explain this apparent paradox partly by arguing that adolescents and adults feel responsible for their character, regardless of their ability to alter specific characteristics, skills, or outcomes. Grade-schoolers, who do not conceive of themselves in terms of a larger personality or character (Inhelder & Piaget, 1958; Selman, 1980; Wood, 1978) are spared this paradox. Rosenberg (1979) reports that 32% of adolescents (14- to 18-year-olds) mentioned general traits, chiefly involving self-control, in discussing feelings of shame; by contrast only 20% of 12- to 13-year-olds and 15% of grade school children (8- to 11-year-olds) mentioned general traits.

For individuals who feel a lack of control and high self-blame, suicide attempts offer a solution: freedom to choose a clear course of action. In choosing "not to be" they may also be attempting to absolve themselves of responsibility and blame for the existence of their character; a character that, they may believe, they are otherwise unable to alter.

SUMMARY

Adolescents see themselves as possessing complex and often conflicting intentions and standards; they seek freedom by unearthing and integrating their real selves. This can lead to rebellion if the adolescent identifies with immediate desires and rejects the conventional, socially sanctioned aspects of self as "phony." Rebellion is often an attempt to escape self-consciousness by participating in gangs, cults, or extremist groups, or by increasing external stimulation, through drug or alcohol abuse or sensation-seeking. Such behaviors draw attention away from the self and away from internal inconsistencies, thus providing a sense of spontaneity and freedom. Rebellion can take on radical prosocial as well as antisocial-delinquent forms.

Depression is the more likely outcome if the adolescent seeks to reject standards but does not feel free to do so, or if the adolescent seeks to reject egotistical intentions but feels unequal to this task because of a perception of the self as weak or as possessing a flawed character. Heightened self-awareness is linked to many of the symptoms of depression. Self-awareness focuses attention on standards, it increases the perceived necessity to live up to them, and it intensifies instances of failure to do so. Efforts to cope with failure by willing away intentions can lead to further failure, increased depression, and anhedonia. For some adolescents, suicide attempts may be seen as a means of increasing freedom and of decreasing characterological self-blame.

NOTES

1. While most studies indicate that self-consciousness leads to helplessness, a few studies indicate that it sometimes has the opposite effect (i.e., invigoration). The former findings are obtained when individuals are made self-conscious about *very large* discrepancies between standards and current behavior; the latter findings emerge when the discrepancies are seen as smaller and more reconcilable (see Carver & Scheier, 1981, for a review).

2. Studies that fail to differentiate between private and public self-consciousness have yielded conflicting age-related findings, but they generally indicate more self-consciousness in adolescence than in middle childhood (Elkind & Bowen, 1979; see Lapsley et al., 1986, for a review).

3. While deindividuation does lead to momentary increases in perceived freedom, we would argue that it detracts from more enduring freedom (see Fromm, 1941). As noted earlier, enduring freedom requires self-regulation as well as absence of restraint. Since deindividuation decreases self-regulation (Carver & Scheier, 1981), the freedom gained is short-lived. Rebellious adolescents who seek this type of freedom must constantly strive to regain it.

PART V

CONCLUSION

12

CONTROL BELIEFS IN CONTEXT

FACTORS INFLUENCING
PSYCHOLOGICAL PROBLEMS

Because of our focus on control beliefs, we have given short shrift to other important determinants of children's psychological problems. In this section we will briefly consider some of these determinants.

Nondevelopmental factors. Mead (1961), Benedict (1934), Erikson (1963) and others have noted the profound influence of culture in shaping children's personality and psychological problems. For example, heightened aggression has been found in societies that sanction and/or reward such behavior (see Mead, 1961) and internalizing problems have been found to be prevalent when the prevailing culture discourages outward expression of feelings (Weisz, Suwanlert, Chiayasit, & Walter, 1987; Weisz, Suwanlert, Chiayasit, Weiss, Achenbach, & Walter, 1987). Other nondevelopmental influences include (a) reinforcement contingencies and exposure to models (Patterson, 1982), (b) temperament (see Berger, 1985), and (c) stress arising from experiences, such as prolonged separation from a parent (Bowlby, 1982; Johnson, 1982), chronic academic failure (Dweck & Elliott, 1983), hospitalization (Melamed & Siegel, 1981) child abuse and neglect (George & Main, 1981), and poverty. There is abundant evidence that stressful (i.e., aversive and uncontrollable) experiences can trigger psychological problems (see Rothbaum, 1980; Wortman & Brehm, 1975; for reviews).

The foregoing factors may, at times, make certain psychological "problems" quite adaptive. For example, in highly competitive societies, aggression may be needed to maintain status or to obtain resources needed for survival. Similarly, depression following a major life stress can allow for a phase of withdrawal to prepare for a fresh adjustment (Brown, 1972; Klinger, 1975; Wortman & Brehm, 1975).

We suspect that the influence of control beliefs is joined by, and often outstripped by, the influence of these other factors in determining the style (i.e., whether it is internalizing or externalizing), incidence and intensity of children's problems.

Developmental factors. We have argued that, as children mature, their changing notions of control help shape developmental changes in the expression of psychological problems. Here we note three other developmental influences: (a) biologically based emotional changes, (b) changes in social context, and (c) developments in cognitive and linguistic competence (e.g., memory, attention, reasoning, speech, and verbal comprehension).

The influence of biology is seen, for example, in the "preparedness" of children at a particular age—their apparent biological readiness—to be fearful of some objects but not others (e.g., small animals but not wooden blocks; see Seligman, 1971). Another biological force, hormonal change in puberty, plays a substantial role in predisposing adolescents to depression (Rutter & Garmezy, 1983; Steinberg, 1981).

Age-related changes in the social context also influence the nature of psychological problems. Consider, for example, the changes in risk factors brought about by lessening of caretaker proximity and surveillance at the end of the toddler period; school entry and increased peer group involvement in middle childhood; availability of drugs and the rights to drive, vote, and work in adolescence.

Cognitive factors such as memory, attention, reasoning, and linguistic skills obviously have an impact on social functioning, but their influence on psychological problems is mediated partly by the kinds of control-related constructs we have described in this book. For example, there are abstract logical principles that are important determinants of adolescent problems, but they are also prerequisites for understanding notions of predictability, contingency, and other control-related constructs. Moreover, children's understanding of control in a particular task is mediated by the demands the task imposes on the children's memory, attention, reasoning, and linguistic skills.

On the other hand, there are many potential explanatory constructs that are cognitive in nature but not directly tied to control beliefs. These include judgments of morality and justice (see Blasi, 1980), interpersonal and self-understanding (Selman, 1980), ability to overcome egocentrism (Elkind, 1979; Higgins, 1981; Mead, 1934) and problem-solving skills

(Spivack & Shure, 1982).[1] While each of these constructs probably adds to the understanding of problems over and above the explanatory power of control constructs, none of them has been shown to account for different types of problems at different ages[2] (see Shantz, 1983).

Moral judgment, for example, has been linked to moral behaviors, including altruism and absence of aggression (see Blasi, 1980), but the purpose of this research has been to show that more morally advanced children have fewer problems, rather than to test whether children of different levels of moral judgment experience different types of problems. Interpersonal reasoning, self-understanding, and problem-solving skills have been linked to an even larger set of personal and interpersonal behaviors, but here too, the focus has not been on accounting for different *types* of problems at different ages. In each of these cases, the research has been designed to show that the more mature the social cognition (e.g., the higher the level of understanding), the more positive (e.g., prosocial, socially competent) the behavior and the fewer the psychological problems. The focus has been on *general* well being and overall psychological problems.

By contrast, research on control has traditionally focused on specific types of problems that follow different developmental trajectories, including phobias (Bandura, 1977), negativism (Brehm, 1981; Wenar, 1982a), inferiority (Dweck & Elliott, 1983), hostile aggression (Wills, 1981), depression (Abramson et al., 1978) and rebellion (Brehm & Brehm, 1982). For this reason, we believe that control is particularly well-suited to serve as an organizing construct in a cognitive-developmental theory of psychological problems.

We know of no research on the *relative causal influence* of the foregoing developmental factors—control beliefs, biological-emotional processes, social context, and noncontrol-related cognitive and linguistic functioning—on age-related changes in the expression of children's problems. It is possible that interactions among these variables account for much of the variance in psychological problems. For example, rebellion and depression may result not just from the separate influences of cognitive development, biology, and social setting, but from feelings about freedom that are associated with hormone-induced energies and increased liberties of puberty (see Rutter & Garmezy, 1983). As another example, inferiority may result from an interaction of perceived control and social setting: awareness of limitations in one's own ability may have little impact in a neutral noncompetitive situation, but a profound impact in a highly evaluative and competitive classroom setting (Nicholls, 1984).

SOME THOUGHTS ON
FUTURE RESEARCH

Testing the ideas offered in this book will require several types of studies. First, we will need more basic epidemiologic developmental research on the prevalence of specific problems at various age levels. Especially valuable would be true longitudinal research tracking the same pool of children across years of development. In planning such research, investigators would do well to recall a point we emphasized earlier: Some studies have failed to find age differences in the prevalence of psychological problems, seemingly because of a reliance on relatively global assessments of problems. Developmental research so finely focused as to distinguish, for example, between phobias of specific objects and general social phobias, and between hostile and instrumental aggression, would provide very useful data.

Ideally, such research should draw reports on children's behavior problems from multiple perspectives—for example, parent reports, teacher reports, reports from trained observers. Extensive research suggests that such multiple informants will show only moderate agreement in their reports of children's problems, and that the closest approach to "truth" about child problems will come through a triangulation of perspectives. (See an excellent review and metaanalysis on this subject by Achenbach, McConaughy, & Howell, 1987.)

One other point should be made regarding developmental research on child problems: To fairly assess age differences in the prevalence of depression and many other problems, it is important to sample groups that have not been preselected for the problem in question. Children who manifest the problem at an atypical age may have high genetic or psychosocial vulnerability to the problem. In examining age differences in depression, for example, some investigators have compared the type and severity of behavioral symptoms across various age groups of children, each previously diagnosed as depressed. Using this research strategy, Kovacs and Paulauskas (1984) found developmental differences that are the opposite of those obtained in certain other studies of depression. Garber (1984), who also used this method, found very few age differences. By contrast, predicted age differences in depression were significant when Garber examined subjects who were not previously diagnosed as depressed. As Kovacs and Paulauskas note, selection of subjects on the basis of a particular problem may introduce bias.

In addition to developmental research on problem prevalence, there is a need for basic research on how children's control-related beliefs change with development. Here, too, longitudinal research would be especially valuable. To study properly the development of control beliefs, we will need "developmentally fair" measures, especially nonverbal measures, that are sensitive to children's differing levels of comprehension (see Garber, 1984). In the absence of such measures, one cannot rule out the possibility that differences in children's endorsements or displays of control concepts reflects "nothing but" differences in general verbal or cognitive skills, and that the latter mediate relations between apparent control beliefs and psychological problems.

At present there are many studies of developments in children's notions of causality and intentionality, but there is little cognitive-developmental research on the larger construct of control per se. Assessments of this construct could draw from Piaget's methods, in which children are presented many carefully designed stimuli and questioned in a systematic but flexible fashion (Inhelder, Sinclair, & Bovet, 1974; Nicholls & Miller, 1984). The combined experimental-task-plus-interview method used to probe children's understanding of ability, effort, task difficulty (Nicholls & Miller, 1984), and chance (Weisz, 1986a) provides a potentially useful starting point for studies on the control construct.

Most of the central ideas put forth in this book represent considerable conceptual stretching—speculation on possible relationships among development, beliefs, and problem behavior, which are only modestly supported by evidence. Ultimately, to test the ideas advanced here, it will be necessary to relate children's developing notions of control to their psychological problems in a direct, empirical fashion. One step in this direction may be research in which children's general level of intellectual functioning is covaried to generate a sharper picture of the relation between control beliefs and psychological problems. Longitudinal designs employing path analysis would shed additional light on causal connections, particularly if children were followed from the beginning to the end of a critical transition—such as the period from 5 to 7 years, or from 12 to 14.

As already noted, many investigators who have related cognitive-developmental constructs to emotional well-being have relied upon global assessments of the latter, such as measures of general adaptiveness or emotional disturbance (e.g., Enright & Sutterfield, 1980; Kurdek,

1980; Noam et al., 1983; Pellegrini, 1985; Selman & Demorest, 1984; Spivak & Shure, 1982; Taylor & Harris, 1984). Other investigators have focused upon a particular psychological problem. For example, several studies examine the link between moral judgment level and degree of delinquency (see Blasi, 1980 for a review).

For present purposes, we would favor a third type of research: Studies that concurrently examine multiple specific problems. When several specific problems are studied at once, it is possible to determine youngsters' relative susceptibility to problems of different types at different levels of cognitive functioning. When a study focuses on a single specific problem, the findings are vulnerable to alternative interpretations, such as that the relationships obtained are owing to nothing but general adaptiveness or cognitive maturity. When a particular form of cognitive functioning is shown to relate to some problems *but not to others* it is easier to rule out these "nothing but" explanations.

Finally, we would suggest that the most convincing demonstrations of causal relationships are often those in which change is produced. If certain kinds of control beliefs do indeed predispose children to certain types of problems, then it may be possible to produce significant change in children's problem behavior by modifying their control-related beliefs through developmentally appropriate interventions. Weisz (1986a) did recently show that children's beliefs in their capacity to control problems at home and at school predicted the extent to which their problems would be ameliorated with psychotherapy. Although suggestive of a general relationship, that study falls short of what we are proposing here in two important respects: (1) It was not focused on control beliefs or problem behavior at the level of specificity that we have proposed, and (2) it did not involve a manipulation aimed at altering control beliefs. Ultimately both kinds of sharpening will be needed if we are to test whether we understand causal processes well enough to produce real change. For those of us whose developmental interests are joined by clinical concerns, the possibility of producing beneficial change is always an intriguing one. In this case, therapeutic benefits would be linked to significant theoretical implications.

SUMMARY

Factors other than control beliefs, such as culture, individual learning history, temperament, and stress, certainly influence the general style, incidence, and intensity of psychological problems.

Changes in biology, social context, and cognitive factors other than control beliefs are important potential determinants of age-related changes in psychological problems. However, control may be particularly well suited to serve as an organizing construct in cognitive-developmental theories of psychological problems. We stress the need for research on all three elements of the proposed model—age-related differences in control, age-related differences in psychological problems, and the relationship between the two. Research linking control beliefs to a variety of specific psychological problems, rather than to a single specific problem or general measures of well being, is most likely to enhance our understanding of the development of psychological problems.

NOTES

1. There are several other social-cognitive constructs that have potential for explaining psychological problems, such as political ideology (e.g., Adelson & O'Neil, 1966) and psychological defense mechanisms (e.g., Chandler, Paget, & Koch, 1978). Earlier in this book we suggested that, insofar as these constructs explain psychological problems, their influence may be mediated by control beliefs.

2. Despite differences between control beliefs and these other domains of social cognition, there are essential commonalities. Moral judgment and control beliefs have in common, among other things, an emphasis on rules and intentions. In fact, we borrow key moral judgment concepts in describing the ages of magic (e.g., absolute rules), power (e.g., norms) and freedom (e.g., internalized standards). An emphasis on emotions and intentions is a common denominator of control beliefs on one hand and interpersonal understanding, self-understanding and egocentrism on the other hand.

3. The Kovacs and Paulauskas findings are also suspect because they indicate decreased incidence of depression after puberty. Several studies have found the opposite pattern (Rutter & Garmezy, 1983). However, this study is methodologically very sound in other respects and serves as a useful model for researchers interested in the relationship between cognitive development and socioemotional functioning.

REFERENCES

Aboud, F. E. (1985). Children's application of attribution principles to social comparisons. *Child Development, 56,* 682-688.

Abramson, L., & Sackeim, M. A. (1977). A paradox in depression: Uncontrollability and self-blame. *Psychological Bulletin, 84,* 838-851.

Abramson, L., Seligman, M., & Teasdale, J. (1978). Learned helplessness in humans: Critique and reformulation. *Journal of Abnormal Psychology, 87,* 49-74.

Achenbach, T. M. (1982). *Developmental psychopathology* (2nd ed.). New York: John Wiley.

Achenbach, T. M., & Edelbrock, C. S. (1981). Behavioral problems and competencies reported by parents of normal and disturbed children aged 4 through 16. *Monographs of the Society for Research in Child Development, 46,* 1-81 (Serial No. 188).

Achenbach, T., & Edelbrock, C. (1983). *Manual for the child behavior checklist and revised child behavior profile.* University of Vermont: Department of Psychiatry.

Achenbach, T. M., McConaughy, S. H., & Howell, C. T. (1987). Child/adolescent behavioral and emotional problems: Implications of cross-informant correlations for situational specificity. *Psychological Bulletin, 101,* 213-232.

Adams, G. R., Abraham, K. G., & Markstrom, C. A. (1987). The relations among identity and development, self-consciousness, and self-focusing during middle and late adolescence. *Developmental Psychology, 23,* 292-297.

Adelson, J. (Ed.). (1980). *Handbook of adolescent psychology,* New York: John Wiley.

Adelson, J., & O'Neil, R. (1966). Growth of political ideas in adolescence: The sense of community. *Journal of Personality and Social Psychology, 4,* 295-306.

Adler, A. (1964). *Superiority and social interest,* Evanston, IL: Northwestern University Press.

Agras, W. S., Sylvester, D., & Oliveau, D. C. (1969). The epidemiology of common fears and phobias. *Comprehensive Psychiatry, 10,* 151-156.

Albert, N., & Beck, A. T. (1975). Incidence of depression in early adolescence: A preliminary study. *Journal of Youth and Adolescence, 4,* 301-308.

Allport, G. (1961). *Pattern and growth in personality.* New York: Holt.

Aman, M. G., & Werry, J. S. (1984). The revised behavior problem checklist in clinic attenders and non-attenders: Age and sex effects. *Journal of Clinical Child Psychology, 13,* 237-242.

Ames, R., Ames, C., & Garrison, W. (1977). Children's causal description for positive and negative interpersonal outcomes. *Psychological Reports, 41,* 595-602.

Angelino, H., Dollins, J., & Mech, E. V. (1956). Trends in the "fears and worries" of school children as related to socio-economic status and age. *Journal of Genetic Psychology, 89,* 263-276.

Anthony, E. J. (1976). Freud, Piaget and human knowledge: Some comparisons and contrasts. In the Chicago Institute for Psychoanalysis (Ed.), *The annual of psychoanalysis* (Vol. 4). New York: International University Press.

Bandura, A. (1977). Self-efficacy: Toward a unifying theory of behavioral change. *Psychological Review, 84,* 191-215.

Bandura, A. (1981). Self-referent thought: A developmental analysis of self-efficacy. In J. H. Flavell & L. Ross (Eds.), *Social cognitive development: Frontiers and possible cognitive futures* (pp. 200-239). Cambridge: Cambridge University Press.

Bandura, A., & Huston, A. C. (1961). Identification as a process of incidental learning. *Journal of Abnormal & Social Psychology, 63,* 311-318.

Barenboim, C. (1981). The development of person perception in childhood and adolescence: From behavioral comparisons to psychological constructs to psychological comparisons. *Child Development, 52,* 129-144.

Bateson, G., Jackson, D. D., Haley, J., & Weakland, J. (1956). Toward a theory of schizophrenia. *Behavioral Science,* 251-264.

Bauer, D. (1976). An exploratory study of developmental changes in children's fears. *Journal of Child Psychology and Psychiatry, 17,* 69-74.

Beaman, A. L., Klentz, B., Diener E. & Svanum, S. (1979). Self-awareness and transgression in children: Two field studies. *Journal of Personality and Social Psychology, 37,* 1835-1846.

Beech, R. P., & Schoeppe, A. (1974). Development of value systems in adolescents. *Developmental Psychology, 10,* 644-656.

Benedict, R. (1934). *Patterns of culture.* New York: Penguin.

Berger, M. (1985). Temperament and individual differences. In M. Rutter, & L. Hersov (Eds.), *Child and adolescent psychiatry* (pp. 3-16). Oxford: Blackwell Scientific.

Berko Gleason, J. (1980, November). The acquisition of routines and social speech. Colloquium presentation at the Eliot-Pearson Department of Child Study, Tufts University, Medford, MA.

Berndt, T. (1982). The features and effects of friendship in early adolescence. *Child Development, 53,* 1447-1460.

Bernstein, R. M. (1980). The development of the self-system during adolescence. *Journal of Genetic Psychology, 136,* 231-245.

Bettelheim, B. (1976). *The uses of enchantment: The meaning and importance of fairy tales.* New York: Random House.

Blasi, A. (1980). Bridging moral cognition and moral action: A critical review of the literature. *Psychological Bulletin, 88,* 1-45.

Blatt, S. (1974). Levels of object representation in anaclitic and introjective depression. *Psychoanalytic Study of the Child, 29,* 107-157.

Bobbitt, B. L., & Keating, D. P. (1983). A cognitive-developmental perspective for clinical research and practice. In P. C. Kendall (Ed.), *Advances in cognitive-behavior research and therapy* (Vol. 2, pp. 198-239). New York: Academic Press.

Boggiano, A. K., & Ruble, D. N. (1979). Competence and the over-justification effect: A developmental study. *Journal of Personality and Social Psychology, 37,* 1462-1468.

Bornstein, B. (1949). Analysis of a phobic child. *Psychoanalytic Study of the Child* (Vols. III-IV, pp. 181-226).

Bowlby, J. (1969). *Disruption of affectional bonds and its effects on behavior.* Canadian Mental Health Supplement (No. 59).

Bowlby, J. (1982). Attachment and loss: Retrospect and prospect. *Journal of Orthopsychiatry, 52,* 664-678.

Brehm, S. S. (1977). The effect of adult influence on children's preference: Compliance versus opposition. *Journal of Abnormal Child Psychology, 5,* 31-41.

Brehm, S. S. (1981). Oppositional behavior in children: A reactance theory approach. In S. S. Brehm, S. M. Kassin, & J. X. Gibbons (Eds.), *Developmental social psychology, theory and research* (pp. 96-121). New York: Oxford University Press.

Brehm, S. S., & Brehm, J. W. (1982). *Psychological reactance: A theory of freedom and control.* New York: Academic Press.

Brickman, P., & Bulman, R. J. (1977). Pleasure and pain in social comparison. In J. Suls & R. Miller (Eds.), *Social comparison processes* (pp. 149-186). Washington, DC: Hemisphere.

Brinton, C. C. (1952). *The anatomy of revolution.* Englewood Cliffs, NJ: Prentice-Hall.

Brockner, J. (1979). Self-esteem, self-consciousness, and task performance: Replications, extension, and possible explanations. *Journal of Personality and Social Psychology, 37,* 447-461.

Brook, J. S., Whiteman, M., Gordon, A. S., & Cohen, P. (1986). Dynamics of childhood and adolescent personality traits and adolescent drug use. *Developmental Psychology, 22,* 403-414.

Broughton, J. (1978). The development of concepts of self, mind, reality and knowledge. In W. Damon (Ed.), *New directions for child development* (Vol. 1). San Francisco: Jossey-Bass.

Brown, F. (1972). Depression and childhood bereavement. In A. Annel (Ed.), *Depressive states in childhood and adolescence* (pp. 35-44). Stockholm: Almqvist & Wikell.

Carroll, J. J., & Steward, M. S. (1984). The role of cognitive development in children's understanding of their own feelings. *Child Development, 55,* 1486-1492.

Cartwright, D. S., Tomson, B., & Schwartz, H. (1975). *Gang delinquency.* Monterey, CA: Brooks/Cole.

Carver, C. S., Blaney, P. H., & Scheier, M. F. (1979). Reassertion and giving up: The interactive role of self-directed attention and outcome expectancy. *Journal of Personality and Social Psychology, 37,* 1859-1870.

Carver, C. S. & Scheier, M. F. (1981). Attention and self-regulation: A control-theory approach to human behavior. New York: Springer-Verlag.

Carver, C., & Scheier, M. (1986). Analyzing shyness: A specific application of broader self-regulatory principles. In W. H. Jones, J. M. Cheek, & S. R. Briggs, (Eds.), *Shyness: Perspectives on research and treatment.* New York: Plenum.

Chandler, M. S., Paget, K. F., & Koch, D. A. (1978). The child's demystification of psychological defense mechanisms: A structural developmental analysis. *Developmental Psychology, 14,* 197-205.

Cloward, R., & Ohlin, L. (1960). *Delinquency and opportunity.* Glencoe, IL: Free Press.

Coie, J. S., & Kupersmidt, J. B. (1983). A behavioral analysis of emerging social status in boys' groups. *Child Development, 54,* 1400-1416.

Covington, M. V., & Omelich, C. L. (1979). The double-edged sword in school achievement. *Journal of Educational Psychology, 71,* 169-182.

Cowan, P. A. (1978). *Piaget with feeling: Cognitive, social and emotional dimensions.* New York: Holt, Rinehart & Winston.

Damon, W. (1977). *The social world of the child.* San Francisco: Jossey-Bass.

Damon, W., & Hart, D. (1982). The development of self-understanding from infancy through adolescence. *Child Development, 53,* 41-64.

Diener, C. I., & Dweck, C. S. (1978). An analysis of learned helplessness: Continuous changes in performance, strategy, and achievement. *Journal of Personality and Social Psychology, 39,* 940-952.

Diener, E. (1979). Deindividuation, self-awareness, and disinhibition. *Journal of Personality and Social Psychology, 36,* 451-462.

Diener, E. (1980). Deindividuation: The absence of self-awareness and self-regulation in group members. In P. B. Paulus (Ed.), *The psychology of group influence.* Hillsdale, NJ: Lawrence Erlbaum.

Diener, E., & Srull, T. K. (1979). Self-awareness, psychological perspective, and self-reinforcement in relation to personal and social standards. *Journal of Personality and Social Psychology, 37,* 413-423.

Diener, E., & Wallbom, M. (1976). Effects of self-awareness, psychological perspective, and self-reinforcement in relation to personal and social standards. *Journal of Personality and Social Psychology, 37,* 413-423.

Dipboye, R. L. (1977). Alternative approaches to deindividuation. *Psychological Bulletin, 84,* 1057-1075.

Dix, T., & Herzberger, S. (1983). The role of logic and salience in the development of causal attribution. *Child Development, 54,* 960-967.

Dodge, K. A. (1983). Behavioral antecedents of peer social status. *Child Development, 54,* 1386-1399.

Dodge, K. A., Schlundt, D. C., Schocken, I., & Delugach, J. D. (1983). Social competence and children's sociometric status: The role of peer group entry strategies. *Merrill-Palmer Quarterly, 29,* 309-336.

Dollinger, S. J., Thelen, M. H., & Walsh, M. L. (1980). Children's conceptions of psychological problems. *Journal of Clinical Child Psychology, 9,* 191-194.

Donaldson, S. K., & Westerman, M. A. (1986). Development of children's understanding of ambivalence and causal theories of emotions. *Developmental Psychology, 22,* 655-662.

Dusek, J. B., Mergler, N. L., & Kermis, M. D. (1976). Attention, encoding and information processing in low- and high-test anxious children. *Child Development, 47,* 201-207.

Dweck, C. S., & Elliott, E. E. (1983). Achievement motivation. In P. Mussen (Ed.), *Handbook of child psychology* (Vol. 4, pp. 643-691).

Dweck, C. S., & Wortman, C. B. (1982). Learned helplessness, anxiety, and achievement motivation: Neglected parallels in cognitive, affective, and coping responses. In H. W. Krohne & L. Laux (Eds.), *Achievement, stress, and anxiety* (pp. 93-125). Washington, DC: Hemisphere.

Elkind, D. (1971). The development of religious understanding in children and adolescents. In M. S. Strommen (Ed.), *Research in religious development* (pp. 655-685). New York: Hawthorne.

Elkind, D. (1974). *Children and adolescents.* New York: Oxford University Press.

Elkind, D. (1979). *The child and society: Essays in applied child development.* New York: Oxford University Press.

Elkind, D., & Bowen, R. (1979). Imaginary audience behavior in children and adolescents. *Developmental Psychology, 15,* 33-44.

Enright, R. D., & Lapsley, D. K. (1981). Judging others who hold opposite beliefs: The development of belief-discrepancy reasoning. *Child Development, 52,* 1052-1063.

Enright, R. D., & Sutterfield, S. J. (1980). An ecological validation of social cognitive development. *Child Development, 51,* 156-161.

Erikson, E. H. (1963). *Childhood and society* (1st ed., 1950). New York: Norton.

Erikson, E. H. (1968). *Identity, youth and crisis.* New York: Norton.

Escalona, S. K. (1983). Basic modes of social interaction: Their emergence and patterning during the first two years of life. *Merrill-Palmer Quarterly, 19,* 205-232.

Feather, N. I. (1980). Values in adolescence. In J. Adelson (Ed.), *Handbook of adolescent psychology.* New York: John Wiley.

Feldman, N. S., & Ruble, D. N. (1981). The development of person perception: Cognitive versus social factors. In S. S. Brehm, S. M. Kassin, & F. X. Gibbons (Eds.), *Developmental social psychology: Theory and research* (pp. 191-206). New York: Oxford University Press.

Fenigstein, A. (1979). Self-consciousness, self-attention, and social interaction. *Journal of Personality and Social Psychology, 37,* 75-86.

Ferguson, T. J., & Rule, B. G. (1980). Effects of inferential set, outcome severity, and basis of responsibility on children's evaluations of aggressive acts. *Developmental Psychology, 16,* 141-146.

Feshbach, S. (1970). Aggression. In P. H. Mussen (Ed.), *Carmichael's manual of child psychology.* New York: John Wiley.

Festinger, L., Pepitone, A., & Newcomb, T. (1952). Some consequences of deindividuation in a group. *Journal of Abnormal and Social Psychology, 47,* 382-389.

Fine, G. A. (1980). The natural history of preadolescent male friendship. In H. C. Foot, A. J. Chapman, & J. R. Smith (Eds.), *Friendship and social relations in children.* Chichester, England: John Wiley.

Fine, G. A. (1981). Friends, impression management, and preadolescent behavior. In S. R. Asher & J. M. Gottman (Eds.), *Friendship and social relations in children.* Chichester, England: John Wiley.

Fishburne, P. M., & Cisin, I. (1980). *National survey on drug abuse: Main findings, 1979.* Rockville, MD: NIMH (NIDA).

Flavell, J. H. (1977). *Cognitive development.* Englewood Cliffs, NJ: Prentice-Hall.

Flavell, J. H. (with Botkin, P. T., Fry, C. L., Jr., Wright, J. W., & Jarvis, P. E.) (1968). *The development of role taking and communication skills in children.* New York: John Wiley.

Fraiberg, S. (1959). *The magic years: Understanding and handling the problems of early childhood.* New York: Scribner's.

Freud, A. (1977). *The ego and the mechanisms of defense.* New York: International University Press.

Freud, S. (1963). *The sexual enlightenment of children.* New York: Macmillan.

Frey, K., & Ruble, D. N. (1985). What children say when the teacher is not around: Conflicting goals in social comparison and performance assessment in the classroom. *Journal of Personality and Social Psychology, 48,* 550-562.

Froming, W. J., Allen, L., & Jensen, R. (1985). Altruism, role-taking, and self-awareness: The acquisition of norms governing altruistic behavior. *Child Development, 56,* 1223-1228.

Fromm, E. (1941). *Escape from freedom.* New York: Reinhart.

Furth, H. (1980). *The world of adults.* New York: Elsevier.

Furth, H., & McConville, K. (1981). Adolescent understanding of compromise in political and social arenas. *Merrill-Palmer Quarterly, 27,* 413-427.

Gallatin, J. (1972). *The development of political thinking in urban adolescents* (National Institute of Education). Washington, DC: U. S. Government Printing Office.

Gallatin, J. (1980). Political thinking in adolescence. In J. Adelson (Ed.), *Handbook of adolescent psychology.* New York: John Wiley.

Gallatin, J., & Adelson, J. (1970). Individual rights and the public good. *Comparative Political Studies, 3,* 226-242.

Garber, J. (1984). The developmental progression of depression in female children. In D. Cicchetti & K. Schneider-Rosen (Eds.), *Childhood depression: New directions for child development* (No. 26). San Francisco: Jossey-Bass.

Gardner, H. (1982). *Developmental psychology* (2nd ed.). Boston: Little, Brown.

Garmezy, N., Masten, A., Nordstrom, L., & Ferrarese, M. (1979). The nature of competence in normal and deviant children. In M. W. Kent & J. E. Rolf (Eds.). *Primary prevention of psychopathology* (Vol. 3, pp. 23-43). Hanover, NH: University Press of New England.

George, C., & Main, M. (1981). Social interactions of young abused children: Approach, avoidance, and aggression. In E. M. Hetherington & R. D. Parke (Eds.), *Contemporary readings in child psychology* (2nd ed.). New York: McGraw-Hill.

Glasberg, R., & Aboud, F. (1982). Keeping one's distance from sadness: Children's self-reports of emotional experiences. *Developmental Psychology, 18,* 287-293.

Gnepp, J. (1983). Children's social sensitivity: Inferring emotions from conflicting cues. *Developmental Psychology, 19,* 805-814.

Gold, M., & Petronio, R. J. (1980). Delinquent behavior in adolescence. In J. Adelson (Ed.), *Handbook of adolescent psychology.* New York: John Wiley.

Gold, M., & Reimer, D. J. (1975). Changing patterns of delinquent behavior among Americans 13 through 16 years old: 1967-1972. *Crime and Delinquency Literature, 7,* 483-517.

Golding, W. (1959). *Lord of the flies.* New York: Capricorn.

Gray-Little, B. (1980). Race and inequity. *Journal of Applied Social Psychology, 10,* 468-481.

Graziano, A. M., DeGiovanni, I. S., & Garcia, K. A. (1979). Behavioral treatment o children's fears: A review. *Psychology Bulletin, 86,* 804-830.

Greenspan, S. T., and Lourie, R. S. (1981). Developmental structuralist approach to th classification of adaptive and pathologic personality organizations: Infancy and earl childhood. *American Journal of Psychiatry, 138,* 725-735.

Griffiths, W. (1952). *Behavior difficulties of children as judged by parents, teachers, an children themselves.* Minneapolis: University of Minnesota Press.

Gruber, H. E., & Voneche, J. J. (Eds.). (1977). *The essential Piaget.* New York: Bas Books.

Guerney, L. F. (1983). Client-centered (nondirective) play therapy. In C. E. Schaeffer K. J. O'Connor (Eds.), *Handbook of play therapy* (pp. 21-64). New York: John Wil

Gunnar-VonGenechten, M. R. (1978). Changing a frightening toy into a pleasant toy allowing the infant to control its action. *Developmental Psychology, 14,* 157-162.

Haan, N., Smith, M. B., & Block, J. (1968). Moral reasoning of young adults: Politi social behavior, family background and personality correlates. *Journal of Persona and Social Psychology, 10,* 183-201.

Haimowitz, M. L. (1966). What price virtue? In M. L. Haimowitz & N. R. Haimo' (Eds.), *Human development: Selected readings* (pp. 2-11). New York: Crowell.

Harlow, L. L., Newcomb, M. D., & Bentler, P. M. (1986). Depression, self-derogat substance use, and suicide ideation: Lack of purpose in life as a mediational fa *Journal of Clinical Psychology, 42,* 5-21.

Harris, P. L., & Olthof, T. (1982). The child's conception of emotion. In G. Butterwo P. Light (Eds.), *Social cognition: Studies of the development of understa* (pp. 188-209). Chicago: University of Chicago Press.

Harris, P. L., Olthof, T., & Terwost, M. M. (1981). Children's knowledge of emotion. *Journal of Child Psychology and Psychiatry and Allied Disciplines, 18,* 15-28.

Harter, S. (1977). A cognitive developmental approach to children's expression of conflicting feelings and a technique to facilitate such expression in play therapy. *Journal of Consulting and Clinical Psychology, 45,* 417-432.

Harter, S. (1981). A model of intrinsic mastery motivation in children: Individual differences and developmental change. *Minnesota Symposium of Child Psychology* (Vol. 14). Hillsdale, NJ: Lawrence Erlbaum.

Harter, S. (1982). A cognitive-developmental approach to children's understanding of affect and trait labels. In F. C. Serafica (Ed.), *Social-cognitive development in context,* (pp. 27-61). New York: Guilford.

Harter, S. (1983). Developmental perspectives on the self-system. In P. H. Mussen (Ed.), *Handbook of child psychology* (Vol. 4, pp. 275-385). New York: John Wiley.

Harter, S., & Buddin, B. J. (1987). Children's understanding of the simultaneity of two emotions: A five stage developmental acquisition sequence. *Developmental Psychology, 23,* 388-399.

Hartup, W. W. (1974). Aggression in childhood: Developmental perspectives. *American Psychologist, 29,* 336-341.

Hartup, W. W. (1983) Peer relations. In P. H. Hussen, *Handbook of child psychology* (Vol. 4, pp. 103-196). New York: John Wiley.

Hawton, K., & Goldacre, M. (1982). Hospital admissions for adverse effects of medicinal agents (mainly self-poisoning) among adolescents in the Oxford region. *British Journal of Psychiatry, 140,* 118-123.

Heckhausen, H. (1981). The development of achievement motivation. In W. W. Hartup (Ed.), *Review of child development research* (Vol 6). Chicago: University of Chicago Press.

Heinstein, M. (1969). *Behavior problems of young children in California.* Berkeley: California Department of Public Health.

Heller, K. A., & Brendt, T. J. (1981). Developmental changes in the formation and organization of personality attributions. *Child Development, 52,* 683-691.

Hersov, L. A., & Berg, I. (Eds.). (1980). *Out of school: Modern perspectives in truancy and school refusal.* Chichester, England: John Wiley.

Hewitt, L. E., & Jenkins, R. L. (1946). *Fundamental patterns of maladjustment: The dynamics of their origin.* Springfield: State of Illinois.

Higgins, E. T. (1981). Role taking and social judgment: Alternative developmental perspectives and processes. In J. H. Flavell & L. Ross (Eds.), *Social cognitive development: Frontiers and possible futures* (pp. 119-153). Cambridge: Cambridge University Press.

Higgins, E. T., & Parsons, J. E. (1983). Social cognition and the social life of the child: Stages as subcultures. In E. T. Higgins, D. N. Ruble, & W. W. Hartup (Eds.), *Social cognition and social development: A sociocultural perspective* (pp. 15-68). New York: Cambridge University Press.

Hull, J. G., & Young, R. D. (1983). Self-consciousness, self-esteem and success-failure as determinants of alcohol consumption in male social drinkers. *Journal of Personality and Social Psychology, 44,* 1097-1109.

Inhelder, B., & Piaget, J. (1958). *The growth of logical thinking from childhood to adolescence.* (A. Parsons & S. Milgram, Trans.). New York: Basic Books.

Inhelder, B., Sinclair, H., & Bovet, M. (1974). *Learning and the development of cognition* (S. Wedwood, Trans.). Cambridge, MA: Harvard University Press.

Janoff-Bulman, R. (1979). Characterological vs. behavioral self-blame: Inquiries into depression and rape. *Journal of Personality and Social Psychology, 37*, 1798-1809.

Jenkins, R. L. (1968). The varieties of children's behavioral problems and family dynamics. *American Journal of Psychiatry, 124*, 1440-1445.

Jersild, A. T., & Holmes, F. B. (1935). *Children's fears*. New York: Teachers College.

Jessor, R., & Jessor, S. L. (1973). A social psychology of marijuana use: Longitudinal studies of high school and college youth. *Journal of Personality and Social Psychology, 26*, 1-15.

Johnson, P. A. (1982). After a child's parent has died. *Child Development, 12*, 160-170.

Johnson, R. D., & Downing, L. L. (1979). Deindividuation and valence of cues: Effects on prosocial and antisocial behavior. *Journal of Personality and Social Psychology, 37*, 1523-1538.

Johnson, S. M., Wahl, G., Martin, S., & Johansson, S. (1973). How deviant is the normal child: A behavioral analysis of the preschool child and his family. In R. D. Rubin, J. P. Brady, & J. D. Henderson (Eds.), *Advances in behavior therapy* (Vol. 4, pp. 37-54). New York: Academic Press.

Kagan, S., & Madsen, M. (1976). Rivalry in Anglo-American and Mexican children of two ages. *Journal of Personality and Social Psychology, 24*, 214-220.

Kandel, D. B., Kessler, R. C., & Margulies, R. Z. (1978). Antecedents of adolescent initiation into stages of drug use: A developmental analysis. In P. B. Kandel (Ed.), *Longitudinal research on drug use: Empirical findings and methodological issues* (pp. 73-99). Washington, DC: Hemisphere.

Kaplan, S. L., Hong, G. K., & Weinhold, C. (1984). Epidemiology of depressive symptomatology in adolescents. *Journal of the American Academy of Child Psychiatry, 23*, 91-98.

Karniol, R. (1978). Children's use of intention cues in evaluating behavior. *Psychological Bulletin, 85*, 76-85.

Karniol, R. (1980). A conceptual analysis of immanent justice responses in children. *Child Development, 51*, 118-130.

Karniol, R. (1985). Children's causal scripts and derogation of the poor: An attributional analysis. *Journal of Personality and Social Psychology, 48*, 791-798.

Keasey, C. B. (1977). Children's developing awareness and usage of intentionality and motives. In H. E. Howe (Ed.), *Nebraska Symposium on Motivation*. Lincoln: University of Nebraska Press.

Kegan, R. (1982). *The evolving self: Problem and process in human development*. Cambridge, MA: Harvard University Press.

Keniston, K. (1967). The sources of student dissent. *Journal of Social Issues, 23*, 108-137.

Klinger, E. (1975). Consequences of commitment to and disengagement from incentives. *Psychological Review, 82*, 1-25.

Knight, G. P., Dubro, A. F., & Chao, C. (1985). Information processing and development of cooperation, competition and individual social values. *Developmental Psychology, 21*, 37-45.

Kohlberg, L. (1969). Stage and sequence: The cognitive developmental approach to socialization. In D. Goslin (Ed.), *Handbook of socialization theory and research* (pp. 347-480). Chicago: Rand McNally.

Kohlberg, L. (1978). The cognitive developmental approach to behavior disorders: A study of the development of moral reasoning in delinquents. In G. Serban (Ed.), *Cognitive defects in the development of mental illness*. New York: Brunner/Mazel.

Koutsourais, H. (1984). Inhibiting magical thought through stories. *Child Study Journal, 14,* 227-236.

Kovacs, M., & Beck, A. T. (1977). An empirical-clinical approach toward a definition of childhood depression. In J. G. Schulterbrant & A. Raskin (Eds.), *Depression in childhood: Diagnosis, treatment, and conceptual models* (pp. 1-26). New York: Raven.

Kovacs, M., & Paulauskas, S. L. (1984). Developmental stage and the expression of depressive disorders in children: An empirical analysis. In D. Cicchetti & K. Schneider-Rosen (Eds.), *Childhood depression.* San Francisco: Jossey-Bass.

Kreitman, N. (1977). *Parasuicide.* London: John Wiley.

Kris, A. O. (1984). The conflicts of ambivalence. In R. S. Eissler, P. B. Neubauer, & A. J. Solnit (Eds.), *The psychoanalytic study of the child, 39,* 213-234. New Haven: Yale University Press.

Kuczynski, L., Radke-Yarrow, M., & Kochanska, G. (1985). *Developmental changes in mother-child interaction during the negativistic period.* Paper presented at the biennial meeting of the Society for Research in Child Development, Toronto.

Kurdek, L. A. (1980). Developmental relations among children's perspective taking, moral judgment, and parent-related behaviors. *Merrill Palmer Quarterly, 26,* 103-121.

Lapouse, R., & Monk, M. A. (1959). Fears and worries in a representative sample of children. *American Journal of Orthopsychiatry, 29,* 803-818.

Lapsley, D. K., Milstead, M., Quintana, S. M., Flannery, D., & Buss, R. R. (1986). Adolescent egocentrism and formal operations: Tests of a theoretical assumption. *Developmental Psychology, 22,* 800-807.

Lazarus, R. S., & Launier, R. (1978). Stress-related transactions between person and environment. In L. A. Pervin & M. Lewis (Eds.), *Perspectives in interactional psychology* (pp. 287-327). New York: Plenum.

Lefcourt, H. M. (1976). *Laws of control: Current trends in theory and research.* Hillsdale, NJ: Lawrence Erlbaum.

Lefkowitz, M. M., & Burton, N. (1978). Childhood depression: A critique of the concept. *Psychological Bulletin, 85,* 716-726.

Lefkowitz, M. M., & Tesiny, E. P. (1985). Depression in children: Prevalence and correlates. *Journal of Consulting & Clinical Psychology, 53,* 647-656.

Levy, D. M. (1972). Oppositional syndromes and oppositional behavior. In S. I. Harrison & J. F. McDermott (Eds.), *Childhood psychopathology: An anthology of basic readings* (pp. 340-359). New York: International University Press.

Lewis, C. C. (1981). How adolescents approach decisions: Changes over grades seven to twelve and policy implications. *Child Development, 52,* 538-544.

Lidz, T. (1964). *The family and human adaptation.* London: Hogarth.

Livesley, W. J., & Bromley, D. B. (1973). *Person perception in childhood and adolescence.* London: John Wiley.

Loeber, R. (1982). The stability of antisocial and delinquent child behavior: A review. *Child Development, 53,* 1431-1446.

Maccoby, E. E. (1980). *Social development: Psychological growth and the parent-child relationship.* New York: Harcourt, Brace, Jovanovich.

Macfarlane, J. W., Allen, L., & Honzik, M. P. (1954). *A developmental study of the behavioral problems of normal children between 21 months and 14 years.* Berkeley, CA: University of California Press.

Mad Magazine Staff. (1983, Winter). The Shadow knows. *Mad Magazine,* p. 42.

Malatesta, C. Z. (1981). Affective development over the lifespan: Involution or growth?. *Merrill-Palmer Quarterly, 27*, 145-173.

Malmquist, C. P. (1983). The functioning of self-esteem in childhood depression. In J. E. Mack & S. L. Ablon (Eds.), *The development and sustenance of self-esteem in childhood* (pp. 189-206). New York: International Universities Press.

Marcia, J. E. (1966). Development and validation of ego identity status. *Journal of Personality and Social Psychology, 3*, 551-558.

Marks, I. M. (1977). Phobias and obsessions. In J. D. Maser, & M.E.P. Seligman (Eds.), *Psychopathology: Experimental models*. San Francisco: W. H. Freedman.

Martin, W. T. (1984). Religiosity and the United States suicide rate, 1972-1978. *Journal of Clinical Psychology, 40*, 1166-1169.

Masterson, J. F. (1967). *The psychiatric dilemma of adolescence*. Boston: Little, Brown.

Matza, D. (1964). *Delinquency and drift*. New York: John Wiley.

Maurer, A. (1965). What children fear. *Journal of Genetic Psychology, 106*, 265-277.

McCabe, A., & Lipscomb, T. (1988). Sex differences in children's verbal aggression. *Merrill-Palmer Quarterly, 34*.

McClintock, C. G., Moskowitz, J. M., & McClintock, E. (1977). Variations in preferences for individualistic, competitive, and cooperative outcomes as a function of age, game, class and task in nursery school children. *Child Development, 48*, 1080-1085.

Mead, G. (1934). *Mind, self, and society*. Chicago: University of Chicago Press.

Mead, M. (Ed.). (1961). *Cooperation and competition among primitive peoples*. Boston: Beacon. (Original work published in 1937)

Meichenbaum, D. H. (1977). *Cognitive-behavior modification*. New York: Plenum.

Melamed, B. G., & Siegel, L. J. (1981). Reduction of anxiety in children facing hospitalization and surgery by use of filmed modeling. In E. M. Hetherington & R. D. Parke (Eds.), *Contemporary readings in child psychology*. New York: McGraw-Hill.

Merelman, R. (1971). The development of policy thinking in adolescents. *American Political Science Review, 65*, 1033-1047.

Miller, A. T. (1985). A developmental study of the cognitive basis of performance impairment after failure. *Journal of Personality and Social Psychology, 49*, 529-538.

Minton, L., Kagan, J., & Levine, J. A. (1971). Maternal control and obedience in the two year old. *Child Development, 42*, 1873-1894.

Minuchin, S. (1974). *Families and family therapy*. Cambridge, MA: Harvard University Press.

Mischel, W., Zeiss, R. & Zeiss, A. (1974). Internal-external control and persistence: validation and implications of the Stanford Preschool Internal-External Scale. *Journal of Personality and Social Psychology, 29*, 265-278.

Montemayor, R., & Eisen, M. (1977). The development of self-conceptions from childhood to adolescence. *Developmental Psychology, 13*, 314-319.

Morris, R. J., & Kratochwill, T. R. (1983). *Treating children's fears and phobias: A behavioral approach*. New York: Pergamon.

Morris, W. N., & Nemeck, D., Jr., (1982). The development of social comparison motivation among preschoolers: Evidence of a stepwise progression. *Merrill-Palmer Quarterly, 28*, 413-425.

Moustakas, C. (1976). *Children in play therapy*. New York: Ballantine.

Murray, D. C. (1973). Suicidal and depressive feelings among college students. *Psychological Reports, 33*, 175-181.

Nelson-Le Gall, S. A. (1985). Motive-outcome matching and outcome foreseeability: Effects on attribution of intentionality and moral judgment. *Developmental Psychology, 21*, 332-337.

Nicholls, J. G. (1976a). Effort is virtuous, but it's better to have ability: Evaluative responses to perceptions of effort and ability. *Journal of Research in Personality, 10,* 306-315.

Nicholls, J. G. (1976b). When a scale measures more than its name denotes: The case of the test anxiety scale for children. *Journal of Consulting and Clinical Psychology, 44,* 976-985.

Nicholls, J. G. (1978). The development of the concepts of effort and ability, perception of academic attainment, and the understanding that difficult tasks require more ability. *Child Development, 49,* 800-814.

Nicholls, J. G. (1979a). Development of perception of own attainment and causal attributions for success and failure in reading. *Journal of Educational Psychology, 71,* 94-99.

Nicholls, J. G. (1979b). Quality and equality in intellectual development: The role of motivation in education. *American Psychologist, 34,* 1071-1084.

Nicholls, J. G. (1984). Achievement motivation: Conceptions of ability, subjective experience, task choice, and performance. *Psychological Review, 91,* 328-346.

Nicholls, J. G. (in press). *Competence and accomplishment: A psychology of achievement motivation.* Cambridge, MA: Harvard University Press.

Nicholls, J. G., & Miller, A. T. (1983). The differentiation of the concepts of difficulty and ability. *Child Development, 54,* 951-959.

Nicholls, J. G., & Miller, A. T. (1984). Reasoning about the ability of self and others: A developmental study. *Child Development, 55,* 1990-1999.

Nicholls, J. G., & Miller, A. T. (1985). Differentiation of the concepts of luck and skill. *Developmental Psychology, 21,* 76-82.

Noam, G. (1985). Stage, phase, and style: The developmental dynamics of the self. In M. Berkowitz & F. Oser (Eds.), *Moral education* (pp. 321-346). Hillsdale, NJ: Lawrence Erlbaum.

Noam, G., Kohlberg, L., & Snarey, J. (1983). Steps toward a model of the self. In B. Lee & G. Noam (Eds.), *Developmental approaches to the self* (pp. 59-141). New York: Plenum.

Nye, C. W., & Carlson, J. S. (1984). The development of the concept of God in children. *Journal of Genetic Psychology, 145,* 137-142.

Nye, F. I. (1975). *Family relationships and delinquent behavior.* Westport, CT: Greenwood.

Olweus, D. (1978). *Aggression in the schools.* Washington: Hemisphere.

Olweus, D. (1988). *Bully/victim problems among school children: Basic knowledge and intervention.* Paper presented at the annual meeting of the American Association for the Advancement of Science, Boston.

Omark, D. R., & Edelman, M. S. (1975). A comparison of status hierarchies in young children: An ethological approach. *Social Sciences Information, 14,* 87-107.

Parsons, J. E. (1974). *Causal attributions and the role of situational cues in the development of children's evaluative judgments.* Unpublished doctoral dissertation, University of California at Los Angeles.

Parsons, J. E., & Ruble, D. N. (1977). The development of achievement-related expectancies. *Child Development, 48,* 1075-1079.

Patterson, G. R. (1982). *Coercive family process.* Eugene, OR: Castalia.

Patterson, G. R., Littman, I., & Brown, T. R. (1968). Negative set and social learning. *Journal of Personality and Social Psychology, 10,* 109-120.

Peevers, B. H., & Secord, P. F. (1973). Developmental changes in attribution of descriptive concepts to persons. *Journal of Personality and Social Psychology, 27,* 120-128.

Pellegrini, D. S. (1985). Social cognition and competence in middle childhood. *Child Development, 56,* 253-264.

Perry, D. G., Perry, L. C., & Rasmussen, P. (1986). Cognitive social learning mediators of aggression. *Child Development, 57,* 700-711.

Peterson, C., Schwartz, S., & Seligman, M. (1981). Self-blame and depressive symptoms. *Journal of Personality and Social Psychology, 41,* 253-259.

Peterson, D. R. (1961). Behavior problems in middle childhood. *Journal of Consulting Psychology, 25,* 205-209.

Piaget, J. (1929). *The child's conception of the world.* Totowa, NJ: Littlefield, Adams.

Piaget, J. (1930). *The child's conception of physical causality.* London: Routledge & Kegan Paul.

Piaget, J. (1948). *The moral judgment of the child.* Glencoe, IL: Free Press.

Piaget, J. (1962). *Play, dreams and imitation.* (H. Gattegano & F. M. Hodgson, Trans.). New York: Norton.

Piaget, J. (1967). Genesis and structure in the psychology of intelligence. In D. Elkind (Ed.), *Six psychological studies by Piaget.* Chicago: Random House.

Piaget, J., & Inhelder, B. (1975). *The origin of the idea of chance in children.* New York: Norton.

Plant, M. (1981). Illicit drug-taking in Britain. In R. Murray, H. Ghodse, C. Harris, S. D. Williams, & P. Williams (Eds.), *The misuse of psychotropic drugs* (pp. 65-69). London: Gaskell—The Royal College of Psychiatrists.

Plath, S. (1966). *The bell jar.* London: Faber & Faber.

Poznanski, E. (1982). The clinical phenomenology of childhood depression. *American Journal of Orthopsychiatry, 52,* 308-313.

Prentice-Dunn, S., & Rogers, R. W. (1982). Effects of public and private self-awareness on deindividuation and aggression. *Journal of Personality and Social Psychology, 43,* 503-513.

Putallaz, M., & Gottman, J. M. (1981). Social skills and group acceptance. In S. R. Asher & J. M. Gottman (Eds.), *The development of children's friendships* (pp. 116-149). Cambridge: Cambridge University Press.

Ralston, N. C., & Thomas, G. P. (1974). *The adolescent: Case studies for analysis.* New York: Chandler.

Rawls, J. A. (1971). *Theory of justice.* Cambridge, MA: Harvard University Press.

Redl, F., & Wineman, D. (1957a). *Children who hate.* Glencoe,IL: Free Press.

Redl, F., & Wineman, D. (1957b). *The aggressive child.* Glencoe, IL: Free Press.

Rholes, W. S., Blackwell, J., Jordon, C., & Walters, C. (1980). A developmental study of learned helplessness. *Developmental Psychology, 16,* 616-624.

Rholes, W. S., & Ruble, D. N. (1984). Children's understanding of dispositional characteristics of others. *Child Development, 55,* 550-560.

Robison, S. M. (1960). *Juvenile delinquency: Its nature and control.* New York: Holt.

Rosen, H. (1985). *Piagetian dimensions of clinical relevance.* New York: Columbia University Press.

Rosenberg, M. (1979). *Conceiving the self.* New York: Basic Books.

Ross, L. (1981). The "intuitive scientist" formulation and its developmental implications. In J. H. Flavell & L. Ross (Eds.), *Social cognitive development: Frontiers and possible futures* (pp. 1-42). Cambridge: Cambridge University Press.

Rotenberg, K. J. (1980). Children's use of intentionality in judgment of character and disposition. *Child Development, 51,* 282-284.

Rotenberg, K. J. (1982). Development of character constancy of self and others. *Child Development, 53,* 505-515.

Rothbaum, F. (1979). Comprehension of the objectivity-subjectivity distinction in childhood and early adolescence. *Child Development, 50,* 1184-1191.

Rothbaum, F. (1980). Children's clinical syndromes and generalized expectations of control. In H. W. Reese & L. P. Lipsett (Eds.), *Advances in child development and behavior* (Vol. 15, pp. 207-246). New York: Academic Press.

Rothbaum, F., & Weisz, J. R. (1988). *Child psychopathology and the development of plans.* Unpublished manuscript, Tufts University.

Rothbaum, F., Weisz, J. R., & Snyder, S. (1982). Changing the world and changing the self: A two-process model of perceived control. *Journal of Personality and Social Psychology, 42,* 5-37.

Rotter, J. B. (1966). Generalized expectancies for internal vs. external control of reinforcement. *Psychological Monographs, 80,* 1-28.

Rotter, J. B., & Mulry, R. C. (1965). Internal vs. external control of reinforcement decision time. *Journal of Personality and Social Psychology, 2,* 598-604.

Ruble, D. N. (1983). The development of social comparison processes and their role in achievement-related self-socialization. In E. T. Higgins, D. N. Ruble, & W. W. Hartup (Eds.), *Social cognition and social development: A sociocultural perspective* (pp. 134-157). New York: Cambridge University Press.

Rutter, M. (1980). *Changing youth in a changing society.* Cambridge, MA: Harvard University Press.

Rutter, M. (1986). Depressive feelings, cognitions, and disorders: A research postscript. In M. Rutter, C. E. Izard, & P. B. Read (Eds.), *Depression in young people: Development and clinical perspectives* (pp. 491-519). New York, London: Guilford.

Rutter, M., & Garmezy, N. (1983). Developmental psychopathology. In P. H. Mussen (Ed.), *Handbook of child psychology* (Vol. 4, pp. 775-912). New York: John Wiley.

Rutter, M., & Giller, H. (1984). *Juvenile delinquency: Trends and perspectives.* Harmondsworth, England: Penguin.

Rutter, M., Graham, P., Chadwick, O.F.D., & Yule, W. (1976). Adolescent turmoil: Fact or fiction. *Journal of Child Psychology and Psychiatry, 17,* 35-56.

Rutter, M., Tizard, J., & Whitmore, K. (1981). *Education, health, and behavior.* Huntington, NY: Krieger. (Originally published in 1970)

Rutter, M., & Yule, W. (1981). Unpublished data reported in M. Rutter & H. Giller (1984), *Juvenile delinquency: Trends and perspectives.* New York: Guilford.

Saarni, C. (1979). Children's understanding of display rules for expressive behavior. *Developmental Psychology, 15,* 424-429.

Saarni, C. (1984). An observational study of children's attempts to monitor their expressive behavior. *Child Development, 55,* 1504-1513.

Salinger, J. D. (1951). *The catcher in the rye.* Boston: Little Brown.

Schulz, C. M. (1966). *Charlie Brown's all-stars.* Cleveland: World.

Schwendinger, H., & Schwendinger, J. S. (1985). *Adolescent subcultures and delinquency.* New York: Praeger.

Seagull, L. M. (1977). *Youth and change in American politics.* New York: Franklin Watts.

Sedlak, A. J., & Kurtz, S. T. (1981). A review of children's use of causal inference principles. *Child Development, 52,* 759-784.

Seiden, R. H. (1969). *Suicide among youth* (U.S. Department of HEW, Public Health Service Publication No. 1971). Washington, DC: U.S. Government Printing Office.

Seligman, M.E.P. (1971). Phobias and preparedness. *Behavior Therapy, 2,* 307-320.

Seligman, M.E.P. (1975). *Helplessness: On depression, development, and death.* San Francisco: Freeman.

Seligman, M.E.P., & Peterson, C. (1986). A learned helplessness perspective on childhood depression: Theory and research. In M. Rutter, C. Izard, & P. B. Read, (Eds), *Depression in young people: Developmental and clinical perspectives.* New York: Guilford.

Selman, R. L. (1979). *Assessing interpersonal understanding: An interview and scoring manual.* Unpublished manuscript, Harvard University.

Selman, R. L. (1980). *The growth of interpersonal understanding: Development and clinical analysis.* New York: Academic Press.

Selman, R. L., & Demorest, A. P. (1984). Observing troubled children's interpersonal negotiation strategies: Implications of and for a developmental model. *Child Development, 55,* 288-304.

Selman, R. L., & Jaquette, D. (1978). Stability and oscillation in interpersonal awareness: A clinical-developmental approach. In C. B. Keasey (Ed.), *Proceedings of the Nebraska Symposium on Motivation: Social cognitive development* (Vol. 25, pp. 261-304). Lincoln, NE: University of Nebraska Press.

Shantz, C. (1975). The development of social cognition. In E. M. Hetherington (Ed.), *Review of child development research* (Vol. 5). Chicago: University of Chicago Press.

Shantz, C. (1983). Social cognition. In *Handbook of child psychology: Cognitive development* (Vol. 3, pp. 495-555). New York: John Wiley.

Shantz, D. W., & Vogdanoff, D. A. (1973). Situational effects on retaliatory aggression at three age levels. *Child Development, 44,* 149-153.

Shapland, J. M. (1978). Self-reported delinquency in boys age 11 to 14. *British Journal of Criminology, 18,* 255-266.

Sharp, K. C. (1982). Preschoolers' understanding of temporal and causal relations. *Merrill-Palmer Quarterly, 28,* 427-436.

Shepherd, M., Oppenheim, B., & Mitchell, S. (1971). *Childhood behavior and mental health.* London: University of London Press.

Shultz, T. R., & Cloghesy, K. (1981). Development of recursive awareness of intention. *Developmental Psychology, 17,* 465-471.

Shultz, T. R., & Ravinsky, F. B. (1977). Similarity as a principle of causal inference. *Child Development, 48,* 1552-1558.

Shultz, T. R., & Wells, D. (1985). Judging the intentionality of action-outcomes. *Developmental Psychology, 21,* 83-89.

Siegler, R. S. (1975). Defining the locus of developmental differences in children's causal reasoning. *Journal of Experimental Child Psychology, 20,* 512-525.

Silver, R. L., & Wortman, C. B. (1980). Coping with undesirable life events. In J. Garber & M.E.P. Seligman, *Human helplessness: Theory and applications.* New York: Academic Press.

Simmonds, R. B. (1977). Conversion or addiction. *American Behavioral Scientist, 20,* 909-924.

Skinner, E. A., & Chapman, M. (1983). *Control beliefs in an action perspective.* Paper presented at the biennial meeting of the Society for Research in Child Development, Detroit.

Sohn, D. (1977). Affect-generating powers of effort and ability—Self attributions of academic success and failure. *Journal of Educational Psychology, 67,* 500-505.

Spivak, G., & Shure, M. B. (1974). *Social adjustment of young children: A cognitive approach to solving real life problems.* San Francisco: Jossey-Bass.

Spivak, G., & Shure, M. B. (1982). The cognition of social adjustment: Interpersonal cognitive problem-solving thinking. In B. B. Lahey & A. E. Kazdin (Eds.), *Advances in clinical child psychology* (Vol. 5, pp. 323-372). New York: Plenum.

Staley, A., & O'Donnell, J. P. (1984). A developmental analysis of mothers' reports of normal children's fears. *Journal of Genetic Psychology, 144,* 165-178.

Staub, E. (1979). *Positive social behavior and morality: socialization and development* (Vol. 2). New York: Academic Press.

Staub, E., & Noerenberg, H. (1981). Property rights, deservingness, reciprocity, friendship: The transitional character of children's sharing behavior. *Journal of Personality and Social Psychology, 40,* 271-189.

Steenbarger, B. N., & Aderman, D. (1979). Objective self-awareness as a non-aversive state: Effect of anticipating discrepancy reduction. *Journal of Personality, 47,* 330-339.

Steinberg, L. D. (1981). Transformations in family relations at puberty. *Developmental Psychology, 17,* 833-840.

Steinhauer, P. D., & Berman, G. (1977). Psychoneurosis, behavior disorders and personality. In P. D. Steinhauer & Q. Rae Grant (Eds.), *Psychological problems of the child and his family* (pp. 137-138). Toronto: Macmillan.

Stipek, D. J. (1981a). Children's perceptions of their own and their classmates' ability. *Journal of Educational Psychology, 73,* 404-410.

Stipek, D. J. (1981b). *Children's use of past performance information in ability and expectancy judgments for self and other.* Paper presented at the meeting of the International Society for the Study of Behavioral Development, Toronto.

Stipek, D. J. (1984). Young children's performance expectations: Logical analysis or wishful thinking? In J. Nicholls (Ed.), *The development of achievement motivation* (pp. 33-56). Connecticut: JAI.

Stipek, D. J., & Hoffman, J. (1980). Development of children's performance-related judgments. *Child Development, 51,* 912-914.

Sullivan, H. S. (1953). *The interpersonal theory of psychiatry.* New York: Norton.

Tarkington, B. (1923). The party. In B. Tarkington, *The fascinating stranger and other stories* (pp. 57-84). Garden City, NY: Doubleday, Page.

Taylor, P. A., & Harris, P. L. (1984). Knowledge of strategies for the expression of emotion among normal and maladjusted boys: A research note. *Journal of Child Psychology & Psychiatry & Allied Disciplines, 25,* 141-145.

Toda, M., Shinotsuka, H., McClintock, C. G., & Stech, F. J. (1978). Development of competitive behavior as a function of culture, age and social comparison. *Journal of Personality and Social Psychology, 36,* 825-839.

Turiel, E. (1974). Conflict and transition in adolescent moral development. *Child Development, 45,* 14-29.

Turiel, E. (1978). The development of concepts of social structure: Social convention. In J. Glick & K. A. Clark-Stewart (Eds.), *The development of social understanding* (pp. 25-108). New York: Gardner.

U.S. Department of Justice (1979). *Crime in the United States, 1978.* Washington, DC: U.S. Government Printing Office.

Ushakov, G. K., & Girich, Y. P. (1972). Special features of psychogenic depressions in children and adolescents. In A. Annell (Ed.), *Depressive states in childhood and adolescence.* Stockholm: Almquist & Wiksell.

Wahl, C. W. (1958). The fear of death. In H. Feifel (Ed.), *The meaning of death* (pp. 16-29). New York: McGraw-Hill.

Wallerstein, J. S., & Kelly, J. B. (1980). *Surviving the breakup: How children and parents cope with divorce.* New York: Basic Books.

Watson, M. W., & Amgott-Kwan, T. (1984). Development of family-role concepts in school-age children. *Developmental Psychology, 20,* 953-959.

Weiner, B., & Graham, S. (1984). An attributional approach to emotional development. In C. Izard, J. Kagan, & R. Zajonc (Eds.), *Emotions, cognition and behavior.* New York: Cambridge University Press.

Weiner, B., Graham, S., Stern, P., & Lawren, M. E. (1982). Using affective cues to infer causal thoughts. *Developmental Psychology, 18,* 278-286.

Weiner, B., & Peter, N. V. (1973). A cognitive-developmental analysis of achievement and moral judgments. *Developmental Psychology, 9,* 290-309.

Weiner, I. B. (1980). Psychopathology in adolescence. In J. Adelson (Ed.), *Handbook of adolescent psychology* (pp. 447-471). New York: John Wiley.

Weiner, I. B. (1982). Case 19: A serious suicide attempt. In I. B. Weiner (Ed.), *Child and adolescent psychopathology* (pp. 443-444). New York: John Wiley.

Weissman, M. M., Orvaschel, H., & Padian, N. (1980). Children's symptom and social functioning self-report scales: Comparison of mothers' and children's reports. *Journal of Nervous and Mental Diseases, 168,* 736-740.

Weisz, J. R. (1980). Developmental change in perceived control: Recognizing non-contingency in the laboratory and perceiving it in the world. *Developmental Psychology, 16,* 385-390.

Weisz, J. R. (1981). Illusory contingency in children at the state fair. *Developmental Psychology, 17,* 481-489.

Weisz, J. R. (1983). Can I control it? The pursuit of veridical answers across the life-span. In P. B. Baltes & O. G. Brim (Eds.), *Life-span development and behavior* (Vol. 5, pp. 233-300). New York: Academic Press.

Weisz, J. R. (1986a). Understanding the developing understanding of control. In M. Perlmutter (Ed.), *Cognitive perspectives on children's social and behavioral development: The Minnesota Symposia on Child Psychology* (Vol. 18, pp. 219-285). Hillsdale, NJ: Lawrence Erlbaum.

Weisz, J. R. (1986b). Contingency and control beliefs as predictors of psychotherapy outcomes among children and adolescents. *Journal of Consulting and Clinical Psychology, 54,* 789-794.

Weisz, J. R., Rothbaum, F., & Blackburn, T. (1984). Standing out and standing in: The psychology of control in America and Japan. *American Psychologist, 39,* 955-969.

Weisz, J. R., & Stipek, D. J. (1982). Competence, contingency, and the development of perceived control. *Human Development, 25,* 250-281.

Weisz, J. R., Suwanlert, S., Chiayasit, W., & Walter, B. R. (1987). Over- and undercontrolled referral problems among children and adolescents from Thailand and the U.S.: The *wat* and *wai* of cultural differences. *Journal of Consulting and Clinical Psychology, 55,* 719-726.

Weisz, J. R., Suwanlert, S., Chiayasit, W., Weiss, B., Achenbach, T. M., & Walter, B. R. (1987). Epidemiology of behavioral and emotional problems among Thai and American children: Parent reports for ages 6-11. *Journal of the American Academy of Child and Adolescent Psychiatry, 26,* 890-897.

Weisz, J. R., Weiss, B., Wasserman, A., & Rintoul, B. (1987). Control-related beliefs and depression among clinic-referred children and adolescents. *Journal of Abnormal Psychology, 96,* 58-63.

Weisz, J. R., Yeates, K. O., Robertson, D., & Beckham, J. C. (1982). Perceived contingency of skill and chance events: A developmental analysis. *Developmental Psychology, 18,* 88-905.

Wenar, C. (1982a). On negativism. *Human Development, 25,* 1-23.

Wenar, C. (1982b). *Psychopathology from infancy through adolescence.* New York: Random House.

Wenar, C. (1984). Commentary: Progress and problems on the cognitive approach to clinical child psychology. *Journal of Consulting and Clinical Psychology, 52,* 57-62.

Wenar, C. (in press). Childhood fears and phobias. In M. Lewis & S. Miller (Eds.), *Handbook of developmental psychopathology.* New York: Plenum.

Werner, H. (1957). The concept of development from a comparative and organismic point of view. In D. Harris (Ed.), *The concept of development* (pp. 125-148). Minneapolis: University of Minnesota Press.

White, R. W. (1960). Competence and the psychosexual stages of development. *Proceedings of the Nebraska Symposium on Motivation* (pp. 97-143). Lincoln: University of Nebraska Press.

White, R. W. (1979). Competence as an aspect of personal growth. In M. W. Kent & J. E. Rolf (Eds.), *Primary prevention of psychopathology* (Vol. 3, pp. 5-22). Hanover, NH: University Press of New England.

Whiting, B. B., & Whiting, J.W.M. (1975). *Children of six cultures.* Cambridge, MA: Harvard University Press.

Wicklund, R. A. (1975). Objective self-awareness. In R. L. Berkowitz (Ed.), *Advances in experimental social psychology* (Vol. 8, pp. 233-277). New York: Academic Press.

Wills, T. A. (1981). Downward comparison principles in social psychology. *Psychological Bulletin, 90,* 245-271.

Wine, J. D. (1982). Evaluation anxiety: A cognitive-attentional construct. In H. W. Krohne, & L. Laux (Eds.), *Achievement, stress and anxiety* (pp. 207-219). Washington, DC: Hemisphere.

Wolff, P. H. (1960). The developmental psychologies of Jean Piaget and psychoanalysis. *Psychological Issues, II*(1) (Monograph 5). New York: International Universities Press.

Wood, M. E. (1978). Children's developing understanding of other people's motives for behavior. *Developmental Psychology, 14,* 561-562.

Wortman, C. B., & Brehm, J. W. (1975). Responses to uncontrollable outcomes: An integration of reactance theory and the learned helplessness model. *Advances in Experimental Social Psychology, 8,* 277-336.

Wylie, R. (1979). *The self-concept* (Vol. 2). Lincoln: University of Nebraska Press.

Yando, R., Seitz, V., & Zigler, E. (1978). *Imitation: A developmental perspective.* Hillsdale, NJ: Lawrence Erlbaum.

Youniss, J. (1980). *Parents and peers in social development: A Sullivan-Piaget perspective.* Chicago: University of Chicago Press.

Zellman, G. L., & Sears, D. O. (1971). Childhood origins of tolerance for dissent. *Journal of Social Issues, 27,* 109-136.

Zigler, E., & Phillips, L. (1961). Psychiatric diagnoses: A critique. *Journal of Abnormal & Social Psychology, 63,* 607-618.

Zimbardo, P. G. (1969). The human choice: Individuation, reason, and order versus deindividuation, impulse, and chaos. In W. J. Arnold, & D. Levine (Eds.), *Proceedings of the Nebraska Symposium on Motivation* (Vol. 17, pp. 237-307). Lincoln: University of Nebraska Press.

NAME INDEX

SUBJECT INDEX

ABOUT THE AUTHORS

Fred Rothbaum is Associate Professor and Chair of the Elliot-Pearson Department of Child Study at Tufts University. He received his Ph.D. from Yale in 1976 and was an Assistant Professor at Bryn Mawr College from 1976 to 1979. He has published several articles dealing with children's social development and parent-child relationships. His current interests are in parent education and developing measures for assessing parent behavior and investigating links between parent behavior and children's social functioning.

John R. Weisz is Professor of Psychology at the University of North Carolina at Chapel Hill, specializing in the child-clinical area. He received his Ph.D. from Yale in 1975 and was an Assistant Professor at Cornell University until 1978. He has also worked as Director of Research and Psychological Services at the Virginia Treatment Center for Children, in Richmond. His research has focused on the development of control beliefs in children, on outcomes of psychotherapy with children, and on the influence of culture on children's behavioral and emotional problems. He is coauthor (with C. Morgan, R. King, and J. Schopler) of *Introduction to Psychology* (7th ed.), McGraw-Hill, 1985.

NOTES

NOTES

NOTES

NOTES

NOTES

NOTES